WATCHMAN

ON THE

WALLS

OF ZION

WATCHMAN

ON THE

WALLS

The Life and Influence of Simon van Velzen

OF ZION

JOSHUA ENGELSMA

REFORMED
FREE PUBLISHING
ASSOCIATION
Jenison, Michigan

Reformed Free Publishing Association
1894 Georgetown Center Drive
Jenison MI 49428
616-457-5970
www.rfpa.org
mail@rfpa.org

Cover design by Christopher Tobias / Tobias Design
Interior design by Katherine Lloyd / theDESKonline.com

ISBN: 978-1-944555-73-3
ISBN: 978-1-944555-74-0 (ebook)
LCCN: 2020950423

To my parents, Kenneth and Pamela Engelsma,
with deep gratitude for their love and support
and for instilling in me a love for the faith of the fathers
by their faithful instruction and example.

CONTENTS

PART 4: PROFESSOR (1854–96)

PREFACE

*M*y journey with Simon van Velzen began during my seminary days. I was nudged in his direction by my dear grandmother, Dena Engelsma. I had the privilege as a child and teenager of living under the same roof as my grandmother, and even after I married and moved out, we still talked frequently. Her interests were mine: God's word, the church, and good books. During one of our visits, she mentioned reading the name of Simon van Velzen but not knowing anything about him. She expressed a desire to know more about the man. Did he have a wife? Children? Interests? I promised her I would do some digging, doubting I would find much.

Shortly thereafter, the seminary faculty licensed me to speak a word of edification in the churches and sent me to Edgerton, Minnesota, for part of the summer. There I did a bit of research and managed to cobble together seven pages of biographical information. Satisfied that I had upheld my promise, I mailed my grandmother the work, including a grainy black-and-white picture of Van Velzen for good measure. As always, Grandma was gracious and thanked me for what I had uncovered.

But the thought of that incomplete sketch ate away at me. I was intrigued by Van Velzen and wanted to know more. My interest was further piqued by a class I took at Calvin Seminary on the theology of Herman Bavinck, a later contemporary of Van Velzen. While there, I dug around in Calvin's immense library and unearthed a few more books on Van Velzen. Slowly, the piece began to develop into an article of respectable length, which was later published in the *Protestant Reformed Theological Journal.*[1]

Satisfied that the journey was over, I buried the project in my filing cabinet. But when I have opened that file through the intervening years, I have been struck again and again by two things: how interesting this man's life was and how little justice I had done to it in the past. So, by bits and pieces over many years, the project has grown into its present form.

◆ ◆ ◆

The driving force behind this journey has always been my conviction that Simon van Velzen occupies an important place in the history of the church of Christ in the nineteenth century. True, he also has a fascinating life. But fascinating details aside, his significance lies in his unswerving conviction for the gospel of grace and the boldness with which he stood for it.

What also amazes me is the fact that his life is essentially a history of the Afscheiding churches. In almost every major event from their beginning in 1834 until their union with Abraham Kuyper's Doleantie in 1892, Van Velzen was involved. The history of these churches needs telling. Surprisingly, there is a dearth of material in English on this history. Most of the available literature ends with the emigrations to America in the 1840s or deals primarily with the social and economic circumstances. Little is written about the ecclesiastical and theological state of affairs. But the importance of knowing this history in order to understand

---

1   Joshua Engelsma, "'Father' van Velzen: The Significance of Simon van Velzen for the Reformation of 1834," *Protestant Reformed Theological Journal* 46, no. 2 (April 2013): 3–47. Without noting every instance, I've adapted parts of that article into this book.

events both in the Netherlands and in America in the twentieth century can hardly be overestimated. And the simple fact that most Reformed churches trace their spiritual heritage back to this reformation makes this history worth reading.

It seems strange, then, that Van Velzen remains largely unknown today. Most works on the Afscheiding mention him only briefly, and almost nothing has appeared in English on his life and work.[2] Where he is mentioned, his influence is largely discredited by an appeal to his forceful character.

I contend that these negative evaluations of Van Velzen's life and influence are incorrect. I intend to demonstrate that, despite his faults, Van Velzen was one of the most significant fathers of the Afscheiding. He was more balanced than most assume, and when he did enter the polemical arena, he did so out of a conviction for the truth and a love for the churches that he served. He was one of the most, if not *the* most, influential leaders in this reformation movement. At best Van Velzen has been largely ignored; at worst his character has been called into question and his influence has been minimized. Both are mistakes.

My sympathies as a biographer are probably obvious. I am not ashamed to say that I view Van Velzen as a spiritual father and do not pretend to approach the subject as an unbiased observer (if such a thing is even possible). George Marsden, in his acclaimed biography of Jonathan Edwards, writes, "Even the fairest observers have biases and blind spots. They have (and they ought to have) interests. The best way to deal with these universal

---

2 One reason why Van Velzen remains largely unknown may be that toward the end of his life he destroyed almost all his personal papers and correspondence. What was left after Van Velzen's death was destroyed by his son-in-law on his orders. Cf. C. Smits, *De Afscheiding van 1834* [The Secession of 1834] (Dordrecht: J. P. van den Tol, 1977), 3:132–33.

phenomena is to acknowledge one's point of view rather than posing as a neutral observer. That way readers can take an author's viewpoint into account, discount it if they wish, and learn from it to the extent they can."[3] I heartily agree.

While biased, I intend to present an accurate portrait of Van Velzen. It was written once of biographers (I paraphrase): "When writing the biography of a man, you first grow to love and respect that person. Then, once you get to know that man's life and character, you despise and detest him. But finally, when you get to the very end, you neither overly love nor overly despise the man, but you begin to understand him and what makes him who he is." I've found this to be the case in my study of Van Velzen, and I believe the perspective I give on his life is accurate.

As you now take up the story of this intriguing individual, I hope you're as fascinated and convicted in reading it as I was in writing it.

---

3   George M. Marsden, *Jonathan Edwards: A Life* (New Haven & London: Yale University Press, 2003), 5.

The Netherlands in 1900
(courtesy of the A. C. Van Raalte Institute, Hope College, Holland, Michigan)

PART 1

YOUTH

(1809–34)

Chapter 1

HOME

S imon van Velzen stood gazing up at a large, familiar building. It was the summer of 1839, and he was in Amsterdam. The building that drew his attention was tucked in among a row of others in an old neighborhood of the capital, the *Jordaan* region, a bit north and west of the city center. Across the threshold of this building ran the *Bloemgracht*, the flower canal, considered by some to be the best and most beautiful of the many navigable waterways that zigzagged through the city like life-giving arteries. From the doorway one was within a stone's throw of the *Westerkerk*, the old Protestant cathedral whose nearly three-hundred-foot spire dominated the skyline and cast a long shadow over the area. Interestingly, it was in another building just a few doors down that a young Jewish girl named Anne Frank hid with her family many years later.

The building of interest to him was a church. A casual observer would have had a hard time recognizing it as such. It looked exactly like all the other buildings on the street, and it certainly did not bear any resemblance to the large, imposing Westerkerk. But it was a church nonetheless—the church, in fact, of which Van Velzen was the new pastor. Although to some Van

Velzen might have appeared an inexperienced young man not yet out of his twenties, he was, in reality, a man with a great deal of wisdom and experience who was highly respected by many in his denomination of churches.

On this particular day Van Velzen was not alone. He was accompanied by his wife—his second, to be precise—and his young son from his first, now-deceased wife. The building interested them too since it was to be their new home. The edifice doubled as a parsonage; in one half of the building Van Velzen would be found on Sundays preaching the gospel to his flock, while in the other half he could be found during the week living with his family.

While the thoughts of wife and child may have strayed to the future, Van Velzen undoubtedly recalled the past. This building had not always been a church. At one point it had been a home. His home. He was born in that building. He had slept in its rooms. He had pressed his face against its windows to see the traffic on street and canal. He had romped through its halls with siblings and friends. On Sundays he had passed solemnly through its door on his way to church and back. Now, after having been gone for a number of years, he would again take up residence there.

Simon van Velzen had come back home.

◆ ◆ ◆

Van Velzen family lore laid claim to ancient nobility and intrigue. The story was told that they were descendants of the Dutch lord Gerard van Velzen (d. 1296). Gerard was involved with several other nobles in a plot to kidnap Count Floris V (1254–96), the beloved "God of the peasants." It was Gerard who finally killed Floris, stabbing him twenty times. His bloody rage was supposedly due to the fact that Floris had raped Gerard's wife, after which the poor woman had committed suicide. Gerard himself was captured, tortured, and quartered as punishment for his part in Floris's death.

If the claims of lineage were indeed true (which they most likely were not), there was little that remained of the wealth and honor of the Van Velzen name in the eighteenth and nineteenth centuries. Simon van Velzen's father, also named Simon van Velzen (1768–1833), was not born to wealth and privilege at some grand, old estate, but in obscurity in a small, out-of-the-way village called Nigtevecht. This quiet hamlet was located ten miles south and east of Amsterdam, nestled into a crook of the Vecht River in the scenic *Vechtstreek* region of the province of Utrecht. The elder Simon was baptized in the Reformed Church there on June 5, 1768. At some point later in life he left that rural setting and moved to the hustle and bustle of Amsterdam.

If the younger Simon was born into any earthly privilege and honor, he had his mother to thank for it, not his father. Johanna Neeltje Geselschap (1776–1865)[1] was born and raised in Amsterdam, but her heritage was German. Her family hailed from the

---

1 Most sources give her name as Neeltje Johanna (cf. Elton J. Bruins, Karen G. Schakel, Sara Fredrickson Simmons, and Marie N. Zingle, *Albertus and Christina: The Van Raalte Family, Home and Roots* [Grand Rapids, MI: William B. Eerdmans Publishing Co., 2004], 208n58; Jaap van Gelderen, *Simon van Velzen: Capita selecta* [Simon van Velzen: Select topics] [Kampen: Vereniging van Oud-Studenten van de Theologische Universiteit Kampen, 1999], 7). But it appears that her name was really Johanna Neeltje. Her son dedicated a book of his collected sermons (*Feeststoffen* [Festival-day themes] [Kampen: S. Van Velzen Jr., 1863]) to his beloved mother "J. N. Geselschap" (cf. C. Trimp, "S. van Velzen als prediker en homileet" ["S. van Velzen as preacher and homiletician"] in *Afscheiding-Wederkeer: Opstellen over de Afscheiding van 1834* [Secession-return: essays on the Secession of 1834], eds. D. Deddens and J. Kamphuis [Haarlem: Vijlbrief, 1984], 224). In addition, Simon named his oldest daughter Johanna Neeltje, undoubtedly after his beloved mother (cf. Van Gelderen, *Simon van Velzen*, 32).

German region of Cleves, where they were well respected by their fellow citizens and consistently occupied public office. Johanna's father emigrated from Germany and established himself as a master painter and glazier in the city of Amsterdam, and in 1777 he became a burgher of the city. Already in Germany the Geselschap family were known adherents to the Reformed faith, so when Johanna's father moved to Amsterdam, he and his family attended the Reformed congregation at the towering Westerkerk. In the fall of 1776, Johanna was born, and she was baptized in the Westerkerk on September 20.

How and when Simon and Johanna met is unknown, but at some point their God-ordained paths crossed. They were joined together as husband and wife in a civil service on April 5, 1799, with the confirmation of their marriage in the church taking place on April 28. They made their home in the building overlooking the Bloemgracht, where together they operated a boarding school. Simon provided the instruction, and Johanna cared for the physical needs of the live-in pupils.

But it was not long before this middle-class couple had their own children to care for and instruct. In all, the Lord would give to Simon and Johanna six children. On December 14, 1809,[2]

---

2 J. A. Wormser, *Karakter en Genade: Het Leven van Simon van Velzen* [Character and grace: the life of Simon van Velzen], vol. 4 of *Een schat in aarden vaten* [A treasure in earthen vessels] (Nijverdal: E. J. Bosch, 1916), 5. J. C. Rullmann mistakenly gives the year of the younger Simon Van Velzen's birth as 1819 (*Christelijke Encyclopaedie voor het Nederlandsche Volk* [Christian encyclopedia for the Dutch people], s.v. "Velzen [Van]"), an error repeated by Ron Gleason in *Herman Bavinck: Pastor, Churchman, Statesman, and Theologian* (Phillipsburg, NJ: P & R Publishing, 2010), 22. F. L. Bos gives the day of his birth as December 25 (*Biografisch lexicon voor de geschiedenis van het Nederlands protestantisme* [Biographical lexicon for the history of Dutch Protestantism], (Kampen: J. H. Kok, 1983), s.v. "Velzen, Simon Van").

Johanna gave birth to the couple's fourth child and second son, whom they named Simon after his father. At that time they were attending one of the local Reformed churches (the *Noorderkerk*), and it was there that young Simon was baptized on December 26 by Rev. Johannes Visch.[3]

◆ ◆ ◆

Young Simon was born at a critical juncture in the history of the Netherlands. The country into which he was born had its origins in the Eighty Years' War, which was waged, with a few intermissions, from 1568 to 1648. The war pitted Spain against seventeen loosely confederated provinces of the Lowlands (modern-day Luxembourg, Belgium, the Netherlands, and northern France). Provoked by persecution from King Philip II of Spain, William of Orange led the provinces in revolt. Although some of the southern provinces fell back into Philip's hands, the seven northernmost provinces (Holland, Zeeland, Friesland, Groningen, Gelderland, Utrecht, and Overijssel) formed the Union of Utrecht in 1579, in which they promised to support one another against Spain. This event is generally regarded as the beginning of the Dutch Republic. In 1609 a truce was reached between the two sides (which permitted the venerable Synod of Dordt to convene), but it was only with the Peace of Westphalia in 1648 that Spain officially recognized the Netherlands as an independent country. Although each liberated province maintained its autonomy, they sent representatives to a national body (called the States General) and recognized an honorary head of state descended from William of Orange (called the Stadtholder). Over the next nearly 150 years,

---

3   At least this is the claim of https://www.genealogieonline.nl/stamboom
   -hobers/I2547.php# (accessed June 16, 2020).

the Dutch enjoyed under the House of Orange a period of peace and great economic prosperity known as the "Golden Age."

In 1795, the Dutch Republic had fallen prey to the French Revolution. Around this time, patriots who were influenced by the revolution to the south came to power in the Netherlands. Disgruntled with the present Stadtholder, William V, whom they viewed as a mere puppet of the English, the revolutionaries forcibly removed William from power and sent him and his family into exile in England. With the House of Orange out of the picture, the Batavian Republic was formed, and the country embraced all things French. In 1806, French dictator Napoleon Bonaparte took control of the Netherlands and placed his brother Louis Napoleon as ruler there. Four years later, Louis Napoleon fell out of favor with his brother and was removed, at which point Napoleon simply annexed the Netherlands as part of France.

Finally, with the defeat of Napoleon in 1813, the Netherlands was liberated. The country recalled the House of Orange from exile and placed William V's son in charge. The Dutch Republic was rechristened the Kingdom of the Netherlands, and William V's son became King William I, the first Dutch monarch.

In time the young boy growing up in the home on the Bloemgracht would come face to face with this heir of the prestigious House of Orange.

◆ ◆ ◆

It was a wonder that Simon lived to see that day.

Conditions in much of the country at the time of his birth were appalling. Disease and poor health were commonplace. The death of family members, though painful, was not altogether unexpected. The infant mortality rate was such that it was not uncommon for parents to have to bury one or more of their own children, something that Simon himself later experienced as a parent.

Matters did not improve with William's accession to the Dutch throne. The disruption of trade during the Napoleonic wars made for an already stagnant economy, but conditions worsened under William's ineptitude. Not all suffered; the rich capitalized on opportunities to become even richer. But the lot of the commoners steadily declined, and more and more could be found roaming the streets and countrysides, homeless and destitute.

Although they too undoubtedly felt a pinch because of the downturn in the economy, the Van Velzens were better off than most. Three identifiable classes existed at that time in Dutch society. The upper class were the wealthy landowners and aristocracy, and the lower class consisted of the destitute. But a strong middle class also existed which was made up of hired hands, poorer farmers, and small tradesmen. The Van Velzens were part of this group. While not fabulously wealthy, they had sufficient means to provide for their daily needs as well as for the education of their children. For instance, many young men who attended university needed outside support to fund their education, but such was not the case with the young Simon. His parents paid 3500 guilders to send their son to university, a sizable sum in that day.[4]

Through these means God was preparing the way for his future calling. Without the financial means to receive a higher education, Simon may never have pursued the gospel ministry at all. But with the funds available to his family, he was able to be prepared for his future labors in the church.

◆ ◆ ◆

---

4 Van Gelderen, *Simon van Velzen*, 9.

Because Simon's life and labors were so closely tied to the church, it is important that the reader know something about the history of the Reformed Church in the Netherlands. This was the church of the Reformation in the Lowlands.

It is generally acknowledged that the Reformation entered this region in four basic stages.[5] First on the scene was Lutheranism. As early as 1518, the teachings of Luther were disseminated among the people of the Lowlands. In fact, the first martyrs of the Reformation were two Dutchmen who were burned at the stake in 1523 for advocating the teachings of the great German reformer. Lutheranism, however, failed to take hold among the Dutch people and never became a popular movement.

The second stage of the Reformation in the Lowlands is often referred to as the "Sacramentarian phase." The "Sacramentarians" were generally a group of educated, upper-class individuals who were dissatisfied with conditions in the Roman Catholic Church. They often gathered in private groups to read and hear the word of God. However, this movement never organized and never established itself in the Netherlands.

Third, the Low Countries were heavily influenced by the Anabaptist movement. Especially during the 1530s and 1540s, the

---

5   For this and what follows, cf. W. Robert Godfrey, "Calvin and Calvinism in the Netherlands," in *John Calvin: His Influence in the Western World*, ed. W. Stanford Reid (Grand Rapids, MI: Zondervan Publishing House, 1982), 95–120; Peter Y. De Jong, "The Rise of the Reformed Churches in the Netherlands," in *Crisis in the Reformed Churches: Essays in Commemoration of the Great Synod of Dort, 1618–1619*, ed. Peter Y. De Jong (Grandville, MI: Reformed Fellowship Inc., 2008), 17–37; Joel R. Beeke, "The Dutch Second Reformation (*Nadere Reformatie*)," *Calvin Theological Journal* 28, no. 2 (November 1993): 298–327; Walter Lagerwey, "The History of Calvinism in the Netherlands," in *The Rise and Development of Calvinism: A Concise History*, ed. John H. Bratt (Grand Rapids, MI: William B. Eerdmans Publishing Co., 1959), 63–102.

Anabaptists gained a large following among the Dutch people. But its members soon descended into radicalism and internal quarrels, leaving many Dutchmen disenchanted with the movement.

The growing unpopularity of Anabaptism prepared the way in the providence of God for the establishment of Calvinism, the fourth and final stage of the Reformation in the Lowlands. The teachings of Calvin took root in the southern part of the Lowlands (present-day Belgium) around 1545, and it was in this region that Reformed churches first sprung up and that the Netherlands (Belgic) Confession was written. A decade or so later, Calvinism spread from there into the northern regions, where it became more firmly established. Thus, the Dutch Reformed church was born.

However, after her conception and subsequent trial-by-fire at the hands of the persecuting Spaniards, the Reformed church in the Lowlands was shaken by the Arminian controversy. Jacobus Arminius (1559–1609) and his followers, often referred to as Remonstrants, wreaked havoc in the churches with their doctrines of conditional election and the freedom of the will. But by the grace of God, the Reformed faith was preserved, and an outstanding victory was won at the great Synod of Dordt (1618–19). With the Canons of Dordt now in place alongside the Confession and the beloved Heidelberg Catechism, the Reformed faith and the truth of salvation by sovereign, particular grace was firmly established in the Netherlands.

Sadly, on the heels of this great victory came a period of doctrinal and moral decay in the church that coincided with her financial and material gains. The winds of the Enlightenment blew powerfully through the church in the later 1700s with devastating effect, so that by the early 1800s she had succumbed almost entirely to wave after wave of modernism and rationalism.

The precious Reformed truths contained in the confessions were forgotten or cast deliberately aside and made a laughingstock.

This sad decay was never more evident than in 1819, the two hundredth anniversary of the Synod of Dordt. The date was almost completely forgotten in the *Hervormde Kerk* (the Dutch name for the state Reformed Church), except by one faithful old preacher, Nicholas Schotsman. He published a work at this time commemorating the great synod and called for the church to return to her Reformed moorings. But rather than provoking shame and repentance, Schotsman's work stirred up hatred and mockery among many in the Hervormde Kerk.[6]

Nicholas Schotsman

Matters in the church were only made worse when William became king. The details of his meddling in the church will be recounted in a later chapter, but suffice it to say that under his watch the church slid even farther down the road of apostasy.

It was into the bosom of this church that Van Velzen was born. And it was this church that he was specially prepared by God to reform.

◆ ◆ ◆

God's preparation of Van Velzen for the work of reformation began in the home. Simon was born to parents who were characterized by a deep, sincere piety. Proof of this is the fact that

6   Peter Y. De Jong, "A Darkness over the Land," in *The Reformation of 1834*, ed. Peter Y. De Jong and Nelson D. Kloosterman (Orange City, IA: Pluim Publishing Inc., 1984), 18–19.

Simon's mother (and presumably his father, before his death) belonged to a conventicle in Amsterdam.[7] Because of the dead orthodoxy that characterized the Reformed church at that time, many hungry souls were left unsatisfied by the preaching Sunday after Sunday. To supplement their spiritual diet, a number of interested persons would meet together in a small group called a conventicle (*gezelschap*), usually at a time on Sunday that did not conflict with the worship services of the church. Together these pious saints would read the scriptures, sing Psalms, and encourage and exhort one another in their godly walk. Frequently they would read selections from the writings of the *oude schrijvers*, older Reformed theologians such as Herman Witsius and Wilhelmus à Brakel. Often a more capable man (called an *oefenaar* or exhorter) would take the lead of the group and read a sermon of an *oude schrijver* or give his own meditation upon a text. The conventicles played an important part in the life of the church at that time: they were the means by which believers were fed and the Reformed faith preserved through decades of spiritual darkness. They were, however, not without their weaknesses. Many conventicles overemphasized the individual's experience and promoted an unhealthy introspection and sickly mysticism. A further danger was that, since believers sought refuge in these inofficial gatherings, the attendees might develop a dim view of the instituted church.

Even while recognizing these dangers, it is safe to see in Simon's parents belonging to a conventicle an indication of their devotion to the Lord—a devotion that could not help but influence their son.

---

7 Eugene P. Heideman, *Hendrik P. Scholte: His Legacy in the Netherlands and in America* (Grand Rapids, MI: William B. Eerdmans Publishing Co., 2015), 130.

Not only was young Simon prepared spiritually in the home, he was also prepared intellectually. He and his siblings received their first years of formal education in their father's boarding school. Through this instruction, Simon's parents soon recognized that God had given exceptional intellectual gifts to their son. Although sharply critical of Van Velzen, Harm Bouwman, a church historian and younger contemporary, grudgingly acknowledged those gifts: "Van Velzen was a man of great gifts and abilities, a man of broad classical education, of great learning, of knowledge and study."[8]

Recognizing these gifts, Simon's parents destined him for the gospel ministry. Knowing that the education in the boarding school would not be sufficient, they provided him with the best education possible. First, they sent their teenage son to the local *gymnasium* (called the *Latijnse School*), a secondary school which trained gifted students for higher education at the university level. The curriculum in these schools was prescribed by royal decree in 1815 and included such subjects as history, geography, mathematics, and mythology. But the primary subject in the curriculum was Latin, since all the instruction in the universities was given in Latin.

After Van Velzen completed his work at the gymnasium in 1827, he was enrolled as one of about 110 students at the *Athenaeum Illustre*. This prestigious preparatory school in the heart of Amsterdam boasted a fine liberal arts curriculum and an exceptional faculty of eleven teachers. Van Velzen sat under men

---

8   Harm Bouwman, *De crisis der jeugd: Eenige bladzijden uit de geschiedenis van de kerken der Afscheiding* [The crisis of youth: Some pages out of the history of the churches of the Secession] (Kampen: J. H. Kok, 1914), 39. All translations from the Dutch in the book are my own, unless otherwise indicated.

such as D. J. van Lennep, J. P. E. Voûte, T. Roorda, and N. G. van Kampen, all renowned scholars in their day. From them, he received instruction in history, mathematics, philosophy, Latin, Greek, Hebrew, and Dutch. These early years were formative ones for Van Velzen. By the means of a godly upbringing in the home and a solid liberal arts education, Van Velzen was prepared by God for his future labors in the church of Jesus Christ.

But something critical was missing. Without question, Van Velzen had the necessary intellectual abilities, but he was lacking the necessary spiritual qualifications: the close walk with God, the depth of spirituality. What he understood with his mind had not sunk deeply into his heart.

It is unknown whether Van Velzen himself actually felt the call at this time to prepare for the ministry. It was not at all uncommon in those days for young men who aspired to the ministry to be devoid of a vibrant spiritual life. Such men saw the office of minister simply as another way of making a living or of pursuing scholarly interests, and nothing more.[9]

This assumed lack in Van Velzen was also evident at the Athenaeum. While the education there was excellent, the moral climate that prevailed was quite the opposite. Many of Van Velzen's fellow students lived riotous, godless lives, and it appears that Van Velzen may have been party to some of their sins at this time. He was acquainted with a handful of other students, including Hendrik Pieter Scholte and Anthony Brummelkamp, who opposed this wickedness and lived upright, God-fearing lives. They were mocked by the other students for their antithetical stance and

---

9 One such young man was Abraham Kuyper, who entered the ministry of the Hervormde Kerk in 1863. Cf. Frank Vanden Berg, *Abraham Kuyper: A Biography* (St. Catherines, Ontario: Paideia Press, 1978), 17–18, 31.

scorned as "Dordtians."[10] Although Scholte and Brummelkamp would play a crucial role in Van Velzen's immediate future, at this time he was not close to them and may have even participated in heaping ridicule upon them.

A significant change was desperately needed. And it would come, in an unexpected time and place.

---

10 Anthony Brummelkamp Jr., *Levensbeschrijving van wijlen Prof. A. Brummelkamp* [Biography of the late Prof. A. Brummelkamp] (Kampen: J. H. Kok, 1910), 21.

Chapter 2

⤏—⊗—⤎

IN THE KING'S
SERVICE

With the completion of his studies at the Athenaeum in 1830, Van Velzen moved from his native Amsterdam to the city of Leiden, twenty miles to the southwest in the province of South Holland. Van Velzen had been accepted at the prestigious University of Leiden, and it was there that Van Velzen would receive his theological training.

His arrival on campus would have met with little attention, not only because of his appearance but because of his character. A nephew of Van Velzen's later wrote of him that he was "known from his student years as a courteous young man with a slim, lithe build and unpretentious manners."[1]

A young Simon van Velzen

However, Van Velzen's studies at Leiden were put on hold shortly after his arrival. A significant event took place that not

---

1   Brummelkamp Jr., *Levensbeschrijving van wijlen Prof. A. Brummelkamp*, 34.

only interrupted his education but also had a tremendous effect on the whole course of his life.

◆ ◆ ◆

That significant event was the Belgian revolt.

For much of their history, the present-day nations of the Netherlands and Belgium were loosely united, commonly identified together as the Lowlands. With the toppling of Napoleon and French power in 1813, the Congress of Vienna met to draw new boundaries and bring stability to Europe. In 1815, the Congress officially united the southern and northern provinces into one kingdom, the United Kingdom of the Netherlands, with William I as its king. The motive of the Congress was to create a

William I

strong country as a buffer to the north of France in hopes of making them think twice before engaging in any future hostilities.

William was agreeable to the idea. In one fell swoop the size of the kingdom over which he reigned was nearly doubled. But the acquisition came at a steep price. In exchange for the southern provinces, the Netherlands was forced to hand over to the British a number of her overseas colonies. As one historian put it, William "traded distant potential for immediate gains."[2]

The arranged marriage of north and south was an unhappy one from the moment the wedding was over. The external unity

---

2   James D. Bratt, *Abraham Kuyper: Modern Calvinist, Christian Democrat* (Grand Rapids, MI: William B. Eerdmans Publishing Co., 2013), 11.

created by aristocratic statesmen miles away masked deep, irreconcilable internal divisions. In the northern provinces, the people spoke the Dutch language, and the Reformed faith was the predominant religion. But in the south, French influence was strong, and Roman Catholicism was the religion of choice. The citizens of the south chafed under the rule of the nominally-Reformed King William. It was only a matter of time before these tensions came to a head.

The problem was exacerbated by William's actions. At times, he put forth the good-faith effort to make things work, even investing a great deal of his own money into the economic development of the two parts of his kingdom, thus launching the industrialization of the south. But at other times, he acted quite foolishly. Historian James Bratt says that William "exuded absolutist airs that contradicted Dutch sensibilities, not to mention the limited monarchy inscribed in the country's new constitution" and "he kept in place the French system of centralized administration." Bratt concludes that William "resemble[s] at once a latter-day enlightened despot and the prototype of the nineteenth-century businessman-king."[3]

The southern provinces were a powder keg waiting to explode. All that was needed was a spark to set off a revolt. Foolishly, William obliged.

The immediate spark of revolution was William's desire to replace Belgian parochial schools with public education. This angered the Catholic Belgians, who responded by collecting some 350,000 signatures in a push for civil liberties. That was in the fall of 1830. William interpreted their response as rebellion and called the Dutch citizenry to arms in order to squash the uprising.

---

3   Bratt, *Abraham Kuyper*, 11.

◆ ◆ ◆

The patriotic masses in the northern Dutch provinces responded eagerly to William's call. In addition to the regular standing army, a number of young men studying at the three major Dutch universities—Leiden, Groningen, and Utrecht—heeded the call and enlisted. The unit culled from the students at Leiden was called the *Vrijwillige Jagers der Leidsche Hoogeschool* (Volunteer Soldiers of Leiden University). Volunteer #202 was the young student Simon van Velzen, who volunteered for the *Jagers* towards the end of October 1830. Despite his differences with King William, he was a patriotic Dutchman and supporter of the House of Orange.

Joining Van Velzen in this unit were two acquaintances from his student days in Amsterdam: Hendrik Scholte and Anthony Brummelkamp.

Volunteer #179 was the bookish, bespectacled Scholte. He was a unique character. He was born in 1805 in Amsterdam to a

family of German immigrants involved in the sugar-refining business. The Scholte men were successful businessmen and had accumulated significant wealth, so that Hendrik was born into the lap of luxury and privilege. The family was also orthodox, although they were Lutheran and not Reformed.

Scholte's life was changed dramatically during his teenage years by a rapid succession of deaths: his father died in 1821, his grandfather in 1822, and his

Hendrik Scholte

mother and brother in 1827. By the time he was twenty-three, Hendrik was the sole heir of the family business. But around that same time, Hendrik left the Lutheran church and joined the Reformed. Feeling called to the ministry, he sold the business and enrolled in Leiden to begin his training. One man described him as a "cultured man, well formed, known from his youth as one in the circle of the Reveil who later associated with many intellectual circles. He was gifted with outstanding gifts of understanding and courage, an impulsive man who as a speaker made a deep impression, an idealist who also had the weakness of his virtues, who was sometimes headstrong and obstinate and sometimes led by the impression of the moment."[4]

Anthony Brummelkamp was Volunteer #38. A native of Amsterdam, he was born in 1811 to Johannes Brummelkamp and his third wife, Anna Henrietta Hes-selink. His mother was from a well-to-do family and received a good education that included learning New Testament Greek. Despite Brummelkamp's instructors at the Athenaeum warning him against associating with Scholte, Anthony became close friends with Hendrik. They encouraged one another in the face of opposition for their godliness, and when Scholte left for

Anthony Brummelkamp

Leiden to prepare for the ministry, Brummelkamp followed him there in 1830.

After enlisting, Van Velzen, Scholte, Brummelkamp, and the 250 other young men of their unit underwent hasty military training on the university grounds for several weeks. By early November, the *Jagers* were ready. They certainly looked the part with their crisp uniforms, their high, tasseled hats, and their bayonet-tipped

---

4   Harm Bouwman, quoted in Heideman, *Hendrik P. Scholte*, 6.

muskets. On November 23, 1830, Van Velzen and his dashing young comrades marched south, along streets lined with patriotic crowds, to face the Belgians.[5]

♦ ♦ ♦

The first assignment of the Jagers was to assist the regulars in the defense of Breda, a significant city in the province of North Brabant and close to the border with Belgium. They were stationed in this area for several months and saw only limited action.

But things got serious for Van Velzen and his fellow soldiers in the summer of 1831 as the war reached its climax. On August 2, King William sent his troops, including the Jagers, on a major offensive into Belgian-held lands, a move later known as the "Ten Days' Campaign." After three days of marching and maneuvering, the Jagers saw their first real taste of action. They were stationed in a potato field near the Belgian village of Beringen when they came under heavy fire from enemy troops. When the guns were silenced and the smoke finally cleared, one of their comrades, Lodewijk Justinus Beeckman from Kampen, lay dead on the ground.

Beeckman's death was the first of three deaths among the Jagers, and it made a deep impression upon Van Velzen and the others. These were, after all, young volunteer students and not career military men, and they were not accustomed to the horrors of the battlefield.

From Beringen they moved deeper into Belgium, arriving on August 13 in the city of Leuven, just outside of Brussels. There

---

5 Melis te Velde, *Anthony Brummelkamp (1811–1888)* (Barneveld: De Vuurbaak, 1988), 38; Van Gelderen, *Simon van Velzen*, 12; Brummelkamp Jr., *Levensbeschrijving van wijlen Prof. A. Brummelkamp*, 24. Brummelkamp says that the unit left on November 23, but Te Velde gives the date of their departure as November 13. For the uniform, cf. Brummelkamp Jr., *Levensbeschrijving van wijlen Prof. A. Brummelkamp*, 24–25.

the Jagers came under heavy cannon fire. Van Velzen dove for cover, and there found himself shoulder-to-shoulder with Brummelkamp. Theirs was a friendship forged in the crucible of war. Despite the fact that they had knocked the Belgians back on their heels, Van Velzen and his unit were ordered to pull out and retreat the very next day. In addition to a sense of relief, there must have also been a sense of frustration. Why were they being ordered to retreat when they had made such deep inroads into Belgium? Why would they fall back when victory was in their grasp?

As it turned out, the Belgians had brought an end to the war, not by their prowess on the battlefield, but by shrewd backroom diplomacy. When they saw that they were nearly overrun, the Belgians sent emissaries to the French and convinced them to come to their aid. Not wanting to risk a war with the powerful French, King William withdrew his troops. The war was over, and the Belgians had gained their independence.

As they trudged back home, Van Velzen and his fellow men-at-arms were hailed as heroes by the Dutch people. In their eyes, the Dutch boys had licked the Belgian rebels and were sent home only because of political wrangling. Raucous crowds lined the streets of Dordrecht, Rotterdam, and Delft as the Jagers marched in what had all the appearance of a victory tour. Van Velzen's unit finally reached Leiden on September 23. An elaborate celebration was held in St. Peterskerk, and all the soldiers received a silver commemorative medal. A year later, on June 22, 1832, Van Velzen and the others were also awarded the Metal Cross in the presence of the king for their bravery.[6]

---

6   Te Velde, *Anthony Brummelkamp*, 39; Van Gelderen, *Simon van Velzen*, 13, 16; Brummelkamp Jr., *Levensbeschrijving van wijlen Prof. A. Brummelkamp*, 25. A picture of the ceremony in St. Peterskerk is found in Van Gelderen, *Simon van Velzen*, 14–15.

In later years, Van Velzen still wore his medals proudly on his chest.

◆ ◆ ◆

Many years later, Van Velzen had opportunity to recall his experiences in the Belgian campaign. During the early years of the Afscheiding, while leading a Sunday morning worship service, Van Velzen was interrupted by a band of soldiers. The soldiers were under orders to call a halt to all such services. They brought Van Velzen into the home of one of the members of the congregation, and five of their number remained behind to guard him closely. Van Velzen later described his interaction with these soldiers: "I had the opportunity then to speak with them about that which I myself had experienced earlier in military service, when with the revolt of Belgium and by the call of the King I discontinued my studies at Leiden University and took up arms to defend the fatherland." In describing the men with whom he fought, he said: "At that time I was witness to many acts of fearlessness and silent courage. But I also saw those who, outside of the danger, acted as the chief spokesmen or sought to give expression in poetry to the heroic fire that glowed within them; or others who did not seem to have any fear before God and men, but, when the enemy came marching up with might, they behaved themselves like cowards." However, Van Velzen was not interested simply in swapping old war stories with the five soldiers: "Above all I desired that these soldiers extol the service of the King of kings."[7]

---

7   Simon van Velzen, "Episode uit den tijd der Kerkelijke Afscheiding in 1836" [Episode out of the time of the ecclesiastical secession in 1836], in *Avondstemmen: Opstellen van wijlen Prof. S. van Velzen* [Evening voices: essays of the late Prof. S. van Velzen] (Leiden: D. Donner, 1897), 137, http://www.neocalvinisme.nl/dv/velzensv/svvavondstemmen.html#p12 (accessed July 16, 2020).

Van Velzen desired the conversion of those soldiers because such a conversion was the profound effect that his own military experience had upon him. One historian says that he returned from the battlefield "a converted man."[8] Van Velzen himself referred to it as his "conversion."[9] His military service was obviously a significant time in his life.

It was significant, first, because Van Velzen's time as a soldier brought him closer to Scholte and Brummelkamp. According to Lubbertus Oostendorp, "Van Velzen was now [after the war] also closer to Scholte than ever. The war had so deepened his spiritual life that while formerly he had been somewhat associated, now he became a zealous member of the group [Scholte Club]."[10] He had been acquainted with these two young men in Amsterdam, but he had not been close to them. Now, after spending many days and experiencing many hardships with them, Van Velzen had developed a strong friendship with Scholte and Brummelkamp.

Second, and more importantly, Van Velzen's experiences in the war brought him closer to God. During the many months of inactivity, Van Velzen devoured the scriptures as well as the writings of Reformed authors. He was especially fond of the German Reformed theologian F. W. Krummacher. The reading of these works and the discussion that followed with Scholte and Brummelkamp served to ground Van Velzen more deeply in the Reformed faith. Several years after the campaign, Van Velzen

---

8 D. H. Kromminga, *The Christian Reformed Tradition: From the Reformation Till the Present* (Grand Rapids, MI: William B. Eerdmans Publishing Co., 1943), 81.

9 Quoted in Jan Wesseling, *De Afscheiding van 1834 in Friesland* [The Secession of 1834 in Friesland] (Groningen: De Vuurbaak, 1981), 2:22; Van Gelderen, *Simon van Velzen*, 16.

10 Lubbertus Oostendorp, *H P Scholte: Leader of the Secession of 1834 and Founder of Pella* (Franeker: T. Wever, 1964), 39.

wrote that during his time as a soldier, "[I] was concerned with my eternal interests." He underwent an intense, spiritual struggle: "While I was examining myself and looking for salvation, I searched the Word of God as I had never done before." The struggle was worth it, because "then to me the way of preservation was opened, then to me the Savior—who was before hidden from me—was revealed with clarity in my heart, and I found in Him my righteousness and strength." The effect was not only the assurance of his salvation, but also a commitment to the truths of the historic Reformed faith. As Van Velzen later described it, "I felt myself also to be in full agreement with the confessions of the church, and I found there my own faith expressed."[11]

This was an important point in God's preparation of Van Velzen for his later calling. Not only did he become wholeheartedly committed to the truth and to the importance of a godly walk, but he also experienced personally the grace of God in his salvation. With this conviction and zeal, Van Velzen took up his studies for the ministry at the University of Leiden. This conviction would be the fire that burned in his belly throughout the rest of his life.

During his time in the service of the king of the Netherlands, God was preparing him for a life of service to a different and greater King. As a soldier in the army of King Jesus, he was to be engaged in a fight for something other than mere acreage in the Lowlands. He was to stand in the breach and battle for the truth of God's word.

---

11 Simon van Velzen, "*Stem eens wachters op Zions muren*" [Voice of a watchman on Zion's walls], in *Kompleete uitgave van de officiëele stukken betreffende den uitgang uit het Nederl. Herv. Kerkgenootschap* [Complete edition of the official documents concerning the exit from the Dutch Reformed Denomination] (Kampen: S. van Velzen Jr., 1863), 2:170, https://babel.hathitrust .org/cgi/pt?id=hvd.ah5w4j&view=1up&seq=9 (accessed July 16, 2020).

Chapter 3

THE CLUB

*B*ack from the battlefield a changed man, Simon was ready to begin in earnest his preparations for the ministry at Leiden.

During the first part of the nineteenth century, the churches did not have a separate seminary as we think of it today, but the theological education was rolled into the public university education. Three major universities existed to serve prospective Dutch ministers: Leiden, Groningen, and Utrecht.

Of the three universities, the University of Leiden could boast the longest and most prestigious history, having been established in 1575 during the illustrious days of the Dutch struggle for independence from Spain under William of Orange. One of the most memorable incidents from this conflict was the siege of Leiden in 1574. The city was surrounded by Spanish troops, and many citizens were dying of starvation. When the people were at the brink of capitulation, the courageous Dutch navy, famously dubbed the "Beggars of the Sea," came to the rescue. They broke through the dikes and flooded the countryside in order to bring their ships to landlocked Leiden. When they arrived, the Spanish forces fled, Leiden was saved, and the Lowlanders gained a much-needed victory. The story goes that, in gratitude for their staunch opposition to the Spaniards, William of Orange offered a reward to the citizens of Leiden. They could choose either perpetual freedom from taxation or to have a university built in their city. The noble Leideners elected to establish a university, and on February 8, 1575, the University of Leiden opened its doors as the first institution of higher learning in the Lowlands.[1]

Thus, the university was more than 250 years old when Van Velzen chose to be trained there for the ministry. It is possible that Scholte and Brummelkamp played a part in his decision to attend Leiden, since they also were enrolled there. But whatever the case may have been, it was at Leiden that God would mold and prepare him for special service in the church of Christ.

On October 3, 1831, the university held a convocation ceremony to mark the commencement of another year of academic labors. Present were 600 full-time students and the 26 professors who taught in the five different academic departments. Van Velzen was in attendance, along with Scholte, Brummelkamp, and the other 150 students enrolled in the theological department, about one-half of all such students in the Netherlands. This made Leiden's theological department the largest in the country.

◆ ◆ ◆

For the next three years, Van Velzen pursued his theological studies under the tutelage of Leiden's four theological professors: Lucas Suringar, Johannes Clarisse, Wessel A. van Hengel, and Nicolaas C. Kist.

---

1   Carl Bangs, *Arminius: A Study in the Dutch Reformation* (Nashville, TN: Abingdon Press, 1971), 45–55; Herman Hanko, *Portraits of Faithful Saints* (Grandville, MI: Reformed Free Publishing Association, 1999), 243.

Lucas Suringar (1770–1833) was responsible for the instruction in dogmatics, natural theology, and the confessions. Van Velzen referred to him later as a "precise" man.[2] Suringar also had a reputation for being a friendly, dutiful, and modest instructor with great abilities, which earned him some recognition in the broader theological community.

Johannes Clarisse (1770–1846) was initially brought to Leiden to teach dogmatics and introductory subjects, but transitioned into teaching apologetics, ethics, hermeneutics, homiletics, pastoral theology, and Old Testament exegesis. He was the most well-known of the theology professors, and Van Velzen described him as "a man, whose colossal knowledge demanded everyone's respect, whose powerful speech controlled the minds, whose charm won all hearts, and sometimes was a highly serious champion of orthodoxy and of pious people of former times."[3]

Wessel A. van Hengel (1779–1871) was the premier exegete of the Leiden faculty. He taught New Testament exegesis and also gave instruction on preaching methods. Van Velzen remembered him as being a sharp, accurate man.[4] He hammered into his students the importance of grammar and accurate, word-for-word explanations of the text. Another former student quipped that Van Hengel had "as much enthusiasm for Greek particles as he did distrust of apostolic ideas."[5] The point was that Van Hengel

---

2 Van Velzen, *"Stem eens wachters op Zions muren,"* 171.
3 Van Velzen, *"Stem eens wachters op Zions muren,"* 2:170. Quoted in Jasper Vree, "The Dominating Theology Within the Nederlandse Hervormde Kerk after 1815 in its Relation to the Secession of 1834," in *Breaches and Bridges: Reformed Subcultures in the Netherlands, Germany, and the United States*, ed. George Harinck and Hans Krabbendam, VU Studies on Protestant History 4 (Amsterdam: VU Uitgeverij, 2000), 36.
4 Van Velzen, *"Stem eens wachters op Zions muren,"* 171.
5 Quoted in Te Velde, *Anthony Brummelkamp*, 41.

believed exegesis should be free from dogmatics; rather, exegesis must form the basis for dogmatics. After Clarisse, Van Hengel had the most influence on the students.

Nicolaas C. Kist (1793–1859) lectured in church history and historical theology. He was a capable instructor whom Van Velzen held in high regard: "For him I had high esteem, particularly because of his understandable instruction."[6]

Although it was widely known that the theological faculty at Leiden was more liberal than the theologians at Utrecht, it was not yet as left-leaning as their counterparts at the University of Groningen. The Groningen theologians, particularly Petrus Hofstede de Groot (1802–86), were on the cutting edge of Dutch theology. They developed what became known as the Groninger School of thought. J. J. van Oosterzee, professor of theology at Utrecht, offered this summary: "Its view of God was unitarian, its doctrine of sin semi-Pelagian; its Christology arian-apollinarian, its entire conception of the Gospel more pedagogically than soteriologically colored; while it lacked any place for a demonology and concluded its eschatology with the doctrine of the restoration of all things."[7] Or, as another modern historian put it, "Christ was less a bleeding Savior than a model of fully realized humanity; the end of religion was less salvation from sin than the achievement of virtue; the human heart was less a sin-blackened seat of evil in need of radical conversion than a trustworthy organ of discernment fit to replace doctrinal standards as the ultimate measure of religious truth."[8]

---

6   Van Velzen, "*Stem eens wachters op Zions muren*," 170–71.

7   Quoted in Hendrik Bouma, *Secession, Doleantie, and Union: 1834–1892*, trans. Theodore Plantinga (Neerlandia, Alberta: Inheritance Publications, 1995), 264. Cf. Bratt, *Abraham Kuyper*, 27–28.

8   James D. Bratt, *Dutch Calvinism in Modern America: A History of a Conservative Subculture* (Grand Rapids, MI: William B. Eerdmans Publishing Co., 1984), 5.

Van Velzen's professors opposed the theology of the Groningen school but in its place taught what was known as "rational supernaturalism." Rational supernaturalism was an endeavor to wed divine revelation with the Enlightenment emphasis upon human reason. It "attempted to reassert traditional Christian doctrines against Enlightenment criticism by appeal to the latter's standards of reason rather than first of all to its own faith or revelation."[9] According to one Scottish visitor to the Netherlands, the result "was a system that affirmed miracles while trying to explain them by nature; that accepted biblical authority without specifying its grounds or particular claims; that acknowledged biblical revelation, though remaining vague as to what exactly Scripture was revealing; that followed Jesus without deciding the question of his two natures."[10] Theirs was a conscious and deliberate movement away from the theology of Calvin and the Synod of Dordt. One historian wrote that "the whole school was controlled by a mild-mannered, polished liberalism."[11]

♦ ♦ ♦

Since his professors were not providing instruction in the Reformed faith that he had come to know and love, Van Velzen turned elsewhere to make up for the deficiency. What he discovered among the throngs of liberal-minded students at Leiden was a handful of young men who were opposed to the theological liberalism and desired the "old paths" of the Reformation and of Dordt.

One of these young men was Brummelkamp, Van Velzen's war buddy and newly acquired friend. The group also included

9   Bratt, *Abraham Kuyper*, 27.
10 Bratt, *Abraham Kuyper*, 27.
11 Oostendorp, *H. P. Scholte*, 37.

George F. Gezelle Meerburg, a mild-mannered young man known as "Snarenberg" to his friends, and Louis Bähler, the son

of a Walloon (French-speaking) minister. But chief among the group was Scholte. Van Velzen and the others were attracted to him because of his age and maturity, and for that reason their group became commonly referred to as the "Scholte Club." This group of students, with the exception of Bähler, who was not a theological student, would later form the nucleus of ministers in the Afscheiding churches.

George F. Gezelle Meerburg

For a little over a year Van Velzen and the other members of the Scholte Club met together. The group assembled to discuss the problems they faced at Leiden and the broader issues facing the Hervormde Kerk. They also read and studied the scriptures together, as well as the writings of the reformers (e.g., Luther and Calvin) and later Reformed theologians (e.g., Wilhelmus á Brakel, Herman Witsius, and F. W. Krummacher).

The Scholte Club often skipped class for their meetings. Scholte, when asked why he refused to attend the lectures of the professors, responded, "I do not have to be taught lying by the professors. I already know how to do that better than they."[12]

Because of their unabashed opposition to the apostasy in the church and university, the club had very little interaction with fellow students, most of whom considered them to be pariahs.

Together the young men of the Scholte Club sought out

---

12 Quoted in Oostendorp, *H. P. Scholte*, 37–38.

others from whom they could learn the Reformed faith. To this end, Van Velzen and his friends soon became acquainted with the Reveil movement in the Netherlands. The Reveil had roots in similar revival movements in Switzerland and France, and it consisted largely of the wealthy and educated. Members met regularly to hear lectures on the Bible and Dutch history, and they decried the moral problems plaguing the country. Still, they were committed members of the state church and opposed any secession from her.

Van Velzen was introduced to Isaac da Costa (1798–1860) and Abraham Jacob Twent van Roosenburg (1799–1868), leading lights in the Reveil, by Scholte, who had been in contact with these men for many years prior. The club also frequently attended the Wednesday and Saturday night meetings of Twent van Roosenburg, where they received insights into the reform movements taking place in other countries.

Isaac da Costa

In addition, Van Velzen and his comrades were influenced by a strand of Dutch piety found in the conventicles (*gezelschappen*). Van Velzen and his friends even frequently attended a conventicle held in the home of a "pious old grain merchant" by the name of Johannes le Feburé (1776–1843), who played a significant role in grounding Van Velzen and the others in the Reformed faith.[13] Three nights every week,

---

13 Robert P. Swierenga and Elton J. Bruins, *Family Quarrels in the Dutch Reformed Churches in the Nineteenth Century*, The Historical Series of the Reformed Church in America 32 (Grand Rapids, MI: William B. Eerdmans

Le Feburé gave instruction on the Bible and the Reformed faith. On any given night somewhere between thirty and eighty people might be crammed into his parlors.

In spite of their unpopularity, almost all the members of the Scholte Club managed to graduate from Leiden before disciplinary action could be taken against them. On October 3 and 4, 1832, Scholte and Meerburg sat for their final examinations. They passed and were declared candidates in the Hervormde Kerk. Scholte was the first to enter officially into the ministry; he was ordained on March 17, 1833, and served the combined congregations of Doeveren and Genderen in the province of North Brabant. Meerburg followed soon thereafter; he was ordained on October 20, 1833, in Almkerk, North Brabant.

The graduation of these two (along with the graduation of Bähler) meant the virtual dissolution of the Scholte Club. The only remaining members were Van Velzen and Brummelkamp, who received a welcome addition to the club that same fall with the arrival of Albertus C. van Raalte. Van Raalte was one of seventeen children of a minister in the Hervormde Kerk. He had initially enrolled in Leiden in 1829 to study medicine, but he had a spiritual awakening when the cholera epidemic struck Leiden in 1832, after which he felt the call to pursue the gospel ministry. His father was a close friend of Prof. Clarisse, and with their help Van Raalte transferred to the theological department to prepare for the ministry.

Van Raalte first came into contact with Van Velzen during the summer of 1832. Van Velzen promptly introduced Van Raalte

---

Publishing Co., 1999), 22; Gerrit J. tenZythoff, *Sources of Secession: The Netherlands Hervormde Kerk on the Eve of the Dutch Immigration to the Midwest*, The Historical Series of the Reformed Church in America 17 (Grand Rapids, MI: William B. Eerdmans Publishing Co., 1987), 130–31.

to Brummelkamp, and the three became close friends. Brummelkamp wrote later, "We found in that young student a wonderful addition."[14]

Despite the welcome addition of Van Raalte, there was little time for lengthy discussions among the three friends. Although they had a less than favorable attitude toward the university, Van Velzen and Brummelkamp still had to pass through Leiden to get into the

Albertus C. Van Raalte

ministry. When Leiden's theology students reached the halfway point of their education, they were required to sit for an examination that would allow them to continue with the second half of their program. Therefore, the two young men were forced to spend that fall studying feverishly.

Van Velzen and Brummelkamp were examined on December 13; both passed *non sine laudibus* (a middle-of-the-road graduation distinction).

But the joy of passing this important exam was soon tempered by a personal loss. In February 1833, Van Velzen's father died in Amsterdam. He was the first of many loved ones whom Simon would have to bring to the grave.

♦ ♦ ♦

It was the spring of 1834, and Van Velzen and Brummelkamp were now ready to graduate from Leiden. But they harbored some doubts about whether they would be allowed to do so. For one thing, the churches were experiencing a stir because of the actions of an orthodox minister named Hendrik de Cock. Although the

---

14 Quoted in Albert Hyma, *Albertus C. Van Raalte and His Dutch Settlements in the United States* (Grand Rapids, MI: William B. Eerdmans Publishing Co., 1947), 31.

two graduates had never been in contact with De Cock, many considered Van Velzen and Brummelkamp to be of the same mindset, so the two students wondered whether they would be allowed to continue.

For another thing, before a theology student was allowed to sit for his final exams, he needed a letter of recommendation from his consistory. After they had moved to Leiden to study, both young men had joined the local Hervormde Kerk (St. Peterskerk), where the aged Rev. Lucas Egeling was pastor. Because of their reputation as part of the Scholte Club, the two friends had some trouble getting the necessary recommendation from the consistory, but eventually the consistory relented, and Van Velzen and Brummelkamp were able to sit for their examination.

The Scholte Club members sat with two other students for their final examination before the Provincial Church Board of South Holland on May 15.[15] The twelve-hour exam was divided into three sessions of four hours each, with the students undergoing examination in their knowledge of scripture, theology, church history, and ethics. One portion of the exam also covered the exegesis of two Old Testament passages (Genesis 22 and 2 Kings 20) and two New Testament passages (Luke 7 and Romans 12).

Van Velzen recalled later that during this examination he spoke freely and openly concerning the doctrine of election as expressed in the Reformed confessions. Those present were shell-shocked at what they heard and conveyed to the young candidate that he could not possibly have learned such things at Leiden! "Certainly not!" was Van Velzen's response. Nevertheless, what he maintained was the historic position of the Reformed churches.

---

15 The Provincial Church Board of South Holland was roughly equivalent to the provincial synod mentioned in the Church Order of Dordt.

Despite this unpopular confession, Van Velzen passed his exam. But his inquisitors could not refrain from politely informing him that when he matured he would have "clearer opinions"; after all, "young men who had initially quite rigid opinions, had showed proofs of a milder view afterwards."[16]

Van Velzen was now a candidate and eligible to receive a call from one of the many congregations in the Hervormde Kerk. The prospects of receiving such a call were not high; at that time there was a surplus of ministers and candidates and not nearly enough pulpits for them all. Yet, Van Velzen would not have to wait long for a call to be extended to him.

But even then, there was controversy.

---

16 Van Velzen, *"Stem eens wachters op Zions muren,"* 2:171–72. Translated in Vree, "Dominating Theology," in *Breaches and Bridges*, 39.

PART 2

REFORMER

(1834–35)

Chapter 4

MARRIAGE AND MINISTRY

T he village of Drogeham was a sleepy, agricultural community nestled among the fields of the northern province of Friesland. At the time of Van Velzen's arrival, the hamlet laid claim to a mere 480 inhabitants, many of whom earned their keep by working the surrounding countryside.

Despite its relatively small size, the hamlet boasted a large, imposing church edifice, which included a bell tower dating back to the Middle Ages. The Hervormde congregation filled the spacious building every Sunday—not only the 480 residents of Drogeham, but also inhabitants of the neighboring villages of Harkema-Opeinde and Buweklooster, for a total of more than 740 souls. Shepherding this large congregation was no small feat for Drogeham's council, which consisted of only four officebearers—two elders and two deacons. Their task was made easier by peace in the church and the absence of troublemakers.

The Hervormde Kerk of Drogeham was once characterized as an "orthodox-experiential congregation."[1] Like many of the

---

1   Wesseling, *De Afscheiding van 1834 in Friesland*, 2:19.

Reformed Church in Drogeham

neighboring Frisian churches, the congregation in Drogeham was a staunch defender of the historic Reformed faith.[2] Prior to the arrival of Van Velzen, the church was served by the Rev. P. D. Koopman, who faithfully proclaimed the gospel of grace. After his departure in 1833, the church struggled to obtain a new pastor because so few ministers in those days heartily maintained the three forms of unity.

But the congregation was also "experiential," which is to say that it contained a mystical strain. Of the 747 members, a mere seven percent (46 members) were actual confessing members. Only this small percentage could claim the necessary experience to partake of the Lord's supper when it was administered, while the large majority lacked such an experience, did not feel the

---

2   Cf. Wesseling, *De Afscheiding van 1834 in Friesland*, 2:20, for evidence of the orthodoxy of many in that part of Friesland. One such example was Rev. T. F. de Haan, who was minister at that time in the town of Ee and later joined the churches of the Afscheiding.

assurance of heart to make confession of their faith, and therefore were kept from partaking of the bread and wine.

At the time of Van Velzen's graduation in the spring of 1834, the Drogeham congregation was on the lookout for a pastor. Recently, they thought they had found one in the Rev. R. W. Duin. However, Duin had been declared mentally unstable and was not able to obtain a doctor's note verifying the soundness of his health, leaving Drogeham in the lurch.[3]

So, on June 29, 1834, the Drogeham congregation extended a call to young Candidate Van Velzen, which he readily accepted. However, he did not receive the approbation of the appropriate church boards until more than four months later. The reason for this extended delay lies in an incident that took place in Drogeham just before Van Velzen's call.

◆ ◆ ◆

Shortly after his graduation from Leiden, Van Velzen was asked to fill the pulpit for the church in Drogeham.[4] He was given the opportunity to lead the morning worship service and another candidate, the brother of an area minister, was asked to do the same in the afternoon. Not only was the congregation receiving pulpit supply, but they were also taking the opportunity to get to know two men whom they might call to be their next pastor.

---

3   Van Gelderen, *Simon van Velzen*, 20; Lutzen H. Wagenaar, *Het "Reveil" en de "Afscheiding": Bijdrage tot de Nederlandsche kerkgeschiedenis van de eerste helft der XIX eeuw* [The "Reveil" and the "Secession": A contribution to Dutch church history of the first half of the nineteenth century] (Heerenveen: J. Hepkema, 1880), 194. Interestingly, Duin would later be the man to replace Van Velzen as pastor of the Secession churches in Friesland.

4   The exact date is unknown, although it was certainly one of the Sundays between May 15 (the day of Van Velzen's examination) and June 29 (the day he received Drogeham's call).

That Sunday morning, Van Velzen delivered an orthodox, edifying sermon that was well-received by the congregation. While the other candidate preached that afternoon, Van Velzen sat listening in the pew reserved for the consistory. The man preached a modernist sermon, one that contrasted sharply with Van Velzen's. "The sermon which he read," Van Velzen later recalled, "was obviously in conflict with the confession that 'we are wholly incapable of doing any good, and inclined to all wickedness' [Heidelberg Catechism, Q 8] and certainly ought not be heard in a Reformed congregation."[5]

So distasteful was the candidate's sermon that many members of the congregation walked out during the middle of the service. Once he noticed members streaming out of the pews, the man quickly finished. After the service, it was customary for the elders to come forward and shake the minister's hand. This was an old, Reformed custom that intended to give expression to the fact that the elders judged the sermon to be in harmony with the confessions. Since Van Velzen was sitting with Drogeham's elders that evening, he followed them out and was expected to extend his right hand to the candidate as well. However, when it came time to shake hands, Van Velzen refused. He objected to the man's liberal preaching and publicly told him so.

It did not take long for the gossip mills to churn. Reports of what Van Velzen had done in the small country church spread like wildfire through Hervormde circles, with a polarizing effect.

On the one hand, some thought that Van Velzen was to be praised for his unflinching stand against false doctrine in the church. The Drogeham congregation was certainly impressed by this orthodox man. So impressed were they that they sent a letter

5   Van Velzen, "*Stem eens wachters op Zions muren,*" 2:173.

to him on June 29 to come over and help them as their new minister, a call which Van Velzen quickly accepted.

Some of Van Velzen's colleagues were also impressed. Several days after the incident in Drogeham, Scholte wrote to De Cock,

> With pleasure I have seen Van Velzen in reform; his actions against a preacher of lies even before he was called show us what the church of God is to expect from him. He stands powerfully for the truth, and the Lord has gifted him with a boldness which the enemies shall find difficult.[6]

On the other hand, some were angered by what Van Velzen had done. When news of what had taken place arrived in Leiden, Rev. Lucas Egeling, pastor of the church to which Van Velzen belonged during his seminary days, raised serious objections to the antics of the young upstart.

Lucas Egeling

"What have I heard!" Egeling scolded. "You refused to extend the hand to a candidate who had preached? It happens to me sometimes that I hear something suggested from the pulpit with which I do not agree, nevertheless I still shake the preacher's hand. This shows humility. Your humility is then known to all men."[7]

On account of Egeling's objections, Van Velzen did not receive the necessary approbation from the ecclesiastical higher-ups. He waited four months after accepting Drogeham's call before the path was

---

6   Quoted in Van Gelderen, *Simon van Velzen*, 21.
7   Van Velzen, "*Stem eens wachters op Zions muren*," 2:174.

finally cleared for him to begin his labors there. Once the call had been approbated, Van Velzen began making plans to leave Leiden.

◆ ◆ ◆

However, before he could move to Drogeham, Van Velzen had other important business to attend to: marriage. His bride-to-be was Johanna Maria Wilhelmina de Moen.

The De Moens were one of the wealthiest families in Leiden. The patriarch, Benjamin de Moen, had made a great deal of money in the textile industry, and he then had the foresight to get out of that business as the market changed, turning instead to real estate. Benjamin had married Johanna Wilhelmina Maria Menzel, a Lutheran from Silesia. She was his third wife, his two previous wives having died suddenly. Together they had nine children, although many of them did not live past infancy. Among their surviving children were a son, Carel, and three daughters: Maria Wilhelmina, Christina Johanna, and Johanna Maria Wilhelmina.

The De Moen children received a fine education. Evidence of this was that they could all speak French, which was considered a hallmark of the educated. They were also brought up as faithful members of the church, catechized by their minister, Rev. Egeling, and influenced by their pious mother.

When Benjamin died in 1824, he left behind a massive fortune to support his widow. When she died in 1831, the now-orphaned children were heirs to a large sum of money. In addition to the money, the youngest daughter, Johanna, also received most of her mother's valuable jewelry, which would be used later to pay the many fines imposed by the government upon her reformer husband.

Simon and his friends would have been acquainted with the De Moen family because they had attended the same church in Leiden and because they had all been frequent attendees at the conventicle of Le Feburé. Formal intro-
ductions were made by Simon's old friend
Meerburg, who was a native of Leiden
and familiar with the family.[8] Van Velzen
and the others quickly befriended Carel
de Moen, a fellow student at Leiden who
would later join them as a leader in the
Afscheiding churches.[9] Carel introduced his
young friends into the De Moen household,
where they were welcomed with open arms.
Like the home of Le Feburé, the De Moen's
became a regular haunt of the Scholte Club.

Carel de Moen

Although they were sure to have enjoyed the stimulating conversation, the young men may have had other motives for their
frequent visits; after all, Carel had three unmarried sisters.

In time, Simon and his friends were betrothed to the three De
Moen women. The eldest daughter, Maria, married Brummelkamp.
Christina, the second daughter, married Albertus van Raalte. And
the youngest of the trio, Johanna, was to be Van Velzen's wife.

---

8   Te Velde, *Anthony Brummelkamp*, 48; Jeanne M. Jacobson, Elton J. Bruins,
    and Larry J. Wagenaar, *Albertus C. Van Raalte: Dutch Leader and Ameri-
    can Patriot* (Holland, MI: Hope College, 1996), 17–18. TenZythoff claims
    that the three met the De Moen family at one of Le Feburé's meetings. Cf.
    Sources of Secession, 130.

9   Carel Godefroi de Moen (1811–79) was a practicing surgeon in the city of
    Hattem who later became a respected minister in the Afscheiding churches
    from 1842 to 1879. Cf. Leonard Sweetman's editorial note in *From Heart to
    Heart: Letters from the Rev. Albertus Christiaan Van Raalte to His Wife, Chris-
    tina Johanna Van Raalte-De Moen, 1836–1847* (Grand Rapids, MI: Heri-
    tage Hall Publications, 1997), 20; Bruins, *Albertus and Christina*, 206–7.

On August 16, 1834, during the narrow window of time between graduation and installation, Simon and Johanna were married, with the confirmation in the church officiated by Rev. Egeling. On the same day, Van Velzen's close friend Brummelkamp married Johanna's oldest sister. Simon Van Velzen was twenty-four years old; his *jevrouw* was seventeen.

Such a situation was not uncommon at that time for an aspiring minister. Undoubtedly, finances played a role in his decision to delay marriage. It may have also been that the student was discouraged from marrying during his seminary days because his focus was supposed to be only on his studies. But, he was strongly encouraged to marry before going into the ministry so as not to raise any suspicions.[10]

Within a few weeks of the marriage, Van Velzen and his new bride moved from Leiden to Drogeham.[11] It must have been quite

---

10 All the other leaders of the Afscheiding followed this marriage track as well. For De Cock, cf. Peter Y. De Jong, "The Dawn of a New Day," in *The Reformation of 1834*, ed. Peter Y. De Jong and Nelson D. Kloosterman (Orange City, IA: Pluim Publishing, 1984), 21–22. For Scholte, cf. Oostendorp, *H. P. Scholte*, 42. For Van Raalte, cf. Hyma, *Van Raalte*, 35. Interestingly, this was the same advice given by Rev. Herman Hoeksema to his students in the Protestant Reformed seminary. Prof. David Engelsma, one of his former students, recalls, "Shortly after I began seminary, Hoeksema made it clear that he strongly disapproved of seminarians marrying while in school: 'It detracts from their studies.' During my last year, with a studied casualness that did not fool me, he indicated that he did not think it wise for a seminary graduate to take a charge unmarried. He spoke vaguely of the possibility of 'talk.'" David J. Engelsma, "I Remember Herman Hoeksema: Personal Remembrances of a Great Man (10)," *Beacon Lights* 50, no. 7 (July 2009): 11.

11 G. Keizer, "*Een paar brieven van wijlen Prof. S. Van Velzen,*" [A few letters of the late Prof. S. van Velzen] *Gereformeerd Theologisch Tijdschrift* [Reformed Theological Journal] 20, no. 11 (March 1920): 400. The following note concerning the membership papers of Johanna Maria was recorded in the Drogeham consistory's minute book: "On November 18 [1834]

an adjustment initially for the young couple. First, they were min-
gling with Frisians, who spoke a different language and maintained
a certain separation from the other provinces. In addition, both
had grown up in large metropolitan areas—Simon in Amsterdam
and Johanna in Leiden—and both belonged to fairly well-to-do
families. Now, they found themselves in a humble little parsonage
on the outskirts of a small, rural hamlet in Friesland.[12] Despite
having to adjust to life in the ministry in Drogeham, Simon and
Johanna looked to the future with excitement and hope.

◆ ◆ ◆

The work began officially on November 9, when Van Velzen was
ordained and installed into the ministry of the Hervormde Kerk by
the moderator Rev. L. D. Westerloo.[13] Van Velzen had originally
asked his close friend Scholte to ordain him, and Scholte came all
the way to Drogeham to do so. But the night before, Scholte told
him, "In the morning I cannot come with you to church, because
I have seceded from the Hervormde denomination."[14] So, Rev.

Johanna Maria Wilhelmina de Moen came here with a certificate of membership from the congregation in Leiden." Cf. T. Dalhuysen, "*De Afscheiding van S. van Velzen*," [The secession of S. van Velzen] *Troffel en Zwaard*
[Trowel and sword], no. 5 (1902): 263, https://www.delpher.nl/nl/boek-
en/view?identifier=MMTUA01:000000413:00003&query=dalhuysen-
+van+velzen+afscheiding&coll=boeken (accessed July 16, 2020).

12 Keizer, "*Een paar brieven van wijlen Prof. S. Van Velzen*," 400. Keizer says,
"The old parsonage was but a humble dwelling a short distance from the
village."

13 Wormser, *Karakter en genade*, 11. Gerrit tenZythoff mistakenly gives the date
of his ordination and installation as October 9 (*Sources of Secession*, 130).

14 Quoted in J. C. Rullmann, *De Afscheiding in de Nederlandsch Hervormde
Kerk der XIXe Eeuw* [The Secession in the Dutch Reformed Church of the
19th century], 2nd ed. (Amsterdam: W. Kirchner, 1916), 187. Scholte
and the congregations of Doeveren and Genderen had seceded from the
Hervormde Kerk on November 1, only a few days before Van Velzen was
ordained (cf. Oostendorp, *H. P. Scholte*, 62–63).

Westerloo was called in to perform the ordination, much to Van Velzen's disappointment.

Van Velzen later recalled his ordination service: "I was kneeling in Drogeham, a village in Friesland. Many ministers surrounded me and stretched the hand of blessing over me. 'Simon son of Jonas, lovest thou me?' said the oldest of them. 'Thus saith the Lord: feed my sheep.' After this speech I arose, but with the feeling that an awfully great work was entrusted to me."[15]

That Sunday afternoon, with his wife and his widowed mother in the audience, Van Velzen preached his inaugural sermon before an overflowing crowd assembled in the Drogeham sanctuary. "On the left-hand side," Van Velzen wrote of the occasion, "I saw my beloved mother, who had not been able to penetrate the large crowd, but I could clearly read on her face that she rejoiced with trembling. And next to her sat my young bride who was so cheerful, so hopeful and joyful to meet the future."[16]

Van Velzen chose as his text the words of the apostle Paul in 1 Corinthians 9:16: "Yea, woe is unto me, if I preach not the gospel!" This was a fitting passage, indicative of the conviction of Van Velzen's heart for the beginning of his work but also for the rest of his difficult ministry.

Van Velzen's labors in Drogeham were that of the typical Reformed minister. He preached twice every Lord's day, with the afternoon service devoted to an exposition of the beloved Heidelberg Catechism. He taught catechism classes for the children of the congregation, chaired the consistory meetings, and tended pastorally to the needs of the sick and grieving members of the

---

15 Quoted in Van Gelderen, *Simon van Velzen*, 22. The ministers present for the laying on of hands were Revs. S. Hogerzeil, J. Lamberts, D. J. Westerloo, and L. D. Westerloo (Wesseling, *De Afscheiding van 1834 in Friesland*, 2:24).
16 Quoted in Van Gelderen, *Simon van Velzen*, 23.

flock. All indications are that Van Velzen was a faithful and energetic pastor to the Drogeham congregation.

Van Velzen had great love for this church of Christ. In later years he remembered the saints there fondly:

> Frequently I thank the Lord that he allowed me to meet especially Jeen Oenes Postma, Wietskemoei, Sjoukjemoei and Sietskemoei. With them I hope hereafter to worship the Lamb in perfection. I can say that I heartily loved the entire congregation, and oh so gladly I could have remained in Drogeham my whole life.[17]

In yet another place he wrote, "I would have gladly and thankfully remained in my relationship to the congregation of Drogeham, where I had been placed according to the evident tokens of the Lord's favor, and where I experienced unforgettable joys."[18]

But such was not the will of God. In a little over a year's time, Van Velzen would leave the Hervormde Kerk and his beloved Drogeham. A reformation was astir, and Van Velzen was right in the thick of it.

---

17 Quoted in W. Van Der Zwaag, *Reveil en Afscheiding: Negentiende-eeuwse kerkhistorie met bijzondere actualiteit* [Reveil and Secession: Nineteenth-century church history with a special theme] (Kampen: De Groot Goudriaan, 2006), 502.

18 Simon van Velzen, "The Apology of the Ecclesiastical Secession in the Netherlands, or A Letter to Mr. G. Groen Van Prinsterer regarding His Opinions Concerning the Secession and the Secessionists," *Protestant Reformed Theological Journal* 45, no. 2 (April 2012): 43.

Chapter 5

———⟫◈⟪———

WATCHMAN ON
THE WALLS OF ZION

*B*efore recounting Van Velzen's break with the Hervormde Kerk, it is necessary to consider briefly the broader reformatory movement of which he was a part.

To do so, we must first introduce Hendrik de Cock.[1] One source described De Cock as "a simple, unassuming, and serious man, a true son of the north, sober, and calm, with an open eye for reality." He possessed a "healthy good sense, frankness, and

---

1   There are three full-length biographies of De Cock, all in Dutch: Helenius de Cock, *Hendrik de Cock, Eerste afgescheiden predikant in Nederland, beschouwd in leven en werkzaamheid* [Hendrik de Cock, first Secession preacher in the Netherlands, considered in life and activity] (Kampen: S. Van Velzen Jr., 1860); J. A. Wormser, *"Werken zoolang het dag is": Het leven van Hendrik de Cock* ["Working while it is day": the life of Hendrik de Cock], vol. 3 of *Een Schat in Aarden Vaten* (Nijverdal: E. J. Bosch, 1915); and Harm Veldman, *Hendrik de Cock (1801–1842): Op de breuklijnen in theologie en kerk in Nederland* [Hendrik de Cock (1801–1842): on the fault lines in theology and church in the Netherlands] (Kampen: J. H. Kok, 2009). For a brief introduction to De Cock in English, cf. Hanko, *Portraits*, 348–57. For a fuller treatment, cf. Marvin Kamps, *1834: Hendrik de Cock's Return to the True Church* (Jenison, MI: Reformed Free Publishing Association, 2014).

Hendrik de Cock

good character."[2] Born in 1801 in Veendam, De Cock studied for the ministry at the University of Groningen, where he fully imbibed the new theology that was sweeping through the churches. After brief pastorates in Eppenhuizen and Noordlaren, he received and accepted the call to serve the little congregation in the town of Ulrum, Groningen. He was installed there by his predecessor, longtime friend, and fellow modernist Petrus Hofstede de Groot.

It was there among the pious congregants of Ulrum that God worked in the heart of De Cock a love for the truth of sovereign grace. One congregant, a simple farmer named Klaas Pieters Kuipenga, told De Cock, "If I must add even one sigh to my salvation, then I would be eternally lost."[3] In the providence of God, De Cock also stumbled across Calvin's *Institutes* and the Canons of Dordt while at Ulrum, neither of which he had read before. He devoured these writings, and soon his preaching began to reflect the truths that they taught. Word of Ulrum's converted minister spread quickly around the countryside, and spiritually-starved people came in droves to hear him preach.

De Cock came into the ecclesiastical crosshairs when he began baptizing the children of those who belonged to other congregations, and also after he publicly and vehemently attacked several liberal colleagues. For this, he was much maligned and persecuted. Finally, on October 13, 1834, De Cock and his consistory

2   Harm Bouwman, quoted in Heideman, *Hendrik P. Scholte*, 6.

3   Engelsma, "The Covenant Doctrine of the Fathers of the Secession," in *Always Reforming: Continuation of the Sixteenth-Century Reformation*, ed. David J. Engelsma (Jenison, MI: Reformed Free Publishing Association, 2009), 101.

composed an "Act of Secession or Return" in which they formally broke off ties with the Hervormde Kerk, declaring her to be a false church.[4] The following evening, 247 members of the Ulrum congregation—an overwhelming majority—joined their consistory in breaking with the mother church in what would be called the Afscheiding (Secession) of 1834.

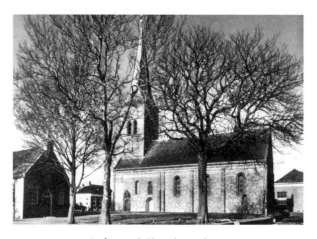

Reformed Church in Ulrum

De Cock and his congregation were not alone for long. They were soon joined by Scholte and his congregation. Scholte was shamefully handled by the Hervormde Kerk for his orthodox stand as well as his close relationship with De Cock, and on October 29, Scholte was suspended by Classis Heusden. Shortly thereafter he and his congregation left the Hervormde Kerk and joined the reformation.

---

4   For a translation of this significant document, cf. the translation by Homer C. Hoeksema in *Always Reforming,* 45–47. The Dutch original can be found in G. Keizer, *De Afscheiding van 1834: Haar aanleiding, naar authentieke brieven en bescheiden beschreven* [The Secession of 1834: Her occasion, according to authentic letters and modest descriptions] (Kampen: J. H. Kok, 1934), 575–76.

◆ ◆ ◆

Van Velzen did not immediately ally himself with De Cock and Scholte. In fact, he and Brummelkamp both were ordained into the Hervormde Kerk after Ulrum had signed the "Act of Secession." Nevertheless, the two ministers were not satisfied with the state of the mother church, nor were they prepared to keep quiet.

Van Velzen expressed his convictions first of all in his preaching. He was known as a capable preacher, and the contents of his sermons in those days stood in sharp contrast to the modernistic, moralistic homilies so prevalent in the Dutch church. Van Velzen proclaimed the precious truths contained in God's word and the Reformed confessions, drawing hundreds of spiritually-starved Dutchmen to Drogeham to be fed. "He began his ministerial career in Drogcham, Friesland," one historian wrote, "where many hundreds came from afar to listen to his soul-stirring sermons. Often because of the multitudes services were conducted in open fields, much as in the early days of the Reformation."[5]

Hette Pieters Hettema, a local Frisian farmer, wrote in his diary that when Van Velzen came to Drogeham, "the testimony went out from him near and far that each Sunday he preached the pure Reformed doctrine of the fathers of Dordt from 1618 and 1619." Hettema added, "This had the result that interested people traveled from long distances away to hear him"—some even traveling for six hours to Drogeham. "There one could hear

---

5   De Jong, "The Dawn of a New Day," 30. The same thing was true of Hendrik de Cock: "The more [De Cock] came to understand the great historic doctrines of God's sovereign and particular grace, the clearer became his sermons as they set forth salvation by grace through faith in Christ and His atoning sacrifice. It is not surprising that, as word of this kind of preaching spread like wildfire through the surrounding countryside, people starving for the Bread of Life streamed to Ulrum to hear De Cock preach." Hanko, *Portraits of Faithful Saints*, 352.

godly, proven men speak who were skilled at judging the truth and were far ahead of me. They knew how to identify the chief points wherein the purity of the doctrine of Rev. van Velzen came out decidedly above that of other so-called orthodox preachers."[6]

◆ ◆ ◆

Like his fellow reformers, Van Velzen expressed concerns about three important areas of life in the church: church government, doctrine, and liturgy.

First, he was dissatisfied with the system of church government that prevailed in the church. This area of the church had deteriorated with the accession of King William to the throne of the Netherlands. Because William had spent some years in exile in England during the French occupation, he was well acquainted with the Anglican Church. Upon his return, the king decided to reorganize the Reformed church along the lines of Anglican polity. On January 7, 1816, William foisted an entirely new system of church government upon the congregations. He even rechristened the church, replacing the old name *Gereformeerde* with the more modern and contemporary title *Hervormde*.

Robert Swierenga, noted historian of this period, explains that William "changed church polity by creating a standing executive committee to run the church and by making delegates to all classes and synods royal appointees. Instead of the revered Dortian polity, the national church now became virtually an administrative arm of the state." He continues, "Given the ever closer bond between church and state, this change meant that

---

6   Hette Piers Hettema, *Nagedachtenis en Levenservaringen, beschreven van H. P. Hettema, oud-ouderling te Beetgum* [Memory and life experiences, described by H. P. Hettema, former elder in Beetgum] (Leeuwarden, 1833), 55–56. Quoted in Van der Zwaag, *Reveil en Afscheiding*, 498.

any future church conflict would inevitably become a threat to the political order. In one stroke the king undermined the historic national church and...further weakened the church and the nation."[7]

Many were happy to accept the changes made by King William. After all, these changes meant that ministers' salaries were being paid again, churches were being repaired, and money was available to support the poor. Who was ready to argue that those were bad things? Very few ministers, since they were "not disposed to bite the hand that fed them."[8]

Van Velzen was one of the few to argue against these changes. He saw them for what they were: hierarchy. He was convinced that the new system infringed upon the kingly rule of Christ over his church. When Van Velzen was later hauled before one of these boards, he was asked point-blank what he thought of King William's system of church government. Van Velzen held nothing back. He candidly responded that the boards were in direct conflict with God's word and the three forms of unity. Shortly thereafter, he was suspended from his office.

◆ ◆ ◆

The second area with which Van Velzen expressed disagreement was the matter of the church's doctrine, particularly her attitude toward the Reformed confessions—the Belgic Confession, the Heidelberg Catechism, and the Canons of Dordt. These sixteenth- and seventeenth-century creeds had been ignored for years and

---

7   Swierenga and Bruins, *Family Quarrels*, 11–12. Cf. also tenZythoff, *Sources of Secession*, 25–42.

8   Albertus Pieters, "Historical Introduction," in *Classis Holland Minutes 1848–1858* (Grand Rapids, MI: Grand Rapids Printing Co., 1943), 11.

were largely unknown by many leaders in the church.[9] Some who were familiar with them mocked them, while many rejected the fundamental truths contained in these documents out-of-hand. These openly denied the Trinity, total depravity, the atonement of Christ, the perfect sinlessness and humanity of Christ, and other cardinal doctrines, about which denial nothing was done.

The position of the church was further weakened by the meddling of King William, especially by his modifying the formula of subscription on July 30, 1816. The formula, in use since the Synod of Dordt, bound ministers and other officebearers to affirm and teach the truths contained in the three forms of unity. Donald Sinnema gives this explanation of William's changes: "Instead of the declaration that the three confessional standards 'do fully agree with the Word of God,' the new version contained a weaker declaration of agreement with 'the doctrine, which, in agreement with God's Holy Word, is contained in the accepted forms of unity.'" Sinnema adds,

> There was deliberate ambiguity in the phrase, "which, in agreement with God's Holy Word," to allow greater freedom on the part of the subscribers. The phrase could be understood either as meaning that the subscriber accepted the doctrine contained in the forms of unity *because (quia)*, or *insofar as (quatenus) it agreed with God's Word.*[10]

---

9   We are told that Hendrik de Cock, prior to his coming to Ulrum, had "never read the creeds of the Reformed Church even though he pledged to teach them faithfully by his official subscription." De Jong, "The Dawn of a New Day," 22.

10   Donald Sinnema, "The Origin of the Form of Subscription in the Dutch Reformed Tradition," *Calvin Theological Journal* 42, no. 2 (November 2007): 279–80. Emphasis is Sinnema's.

With this subtle change, William opened the doors of the church to all sorts of heretical and erroneous interpretations of the creeds.

Van Velzen later recalled, "The churches continued to be entrusted to public opponents of the faith of the Reformed church, to mockers of the creeds, and to those who denied the truth, whose rejection of the truth scorns God himself, and for which truth our fathers willingly abandoned their possessions and life itself."[11]

Van Velzen was opposed to this disregard for and disparagement of the historic Reformed confessions. He wanted the Hervormde Kerk to restore faithful adherence to these creeds. Before he had even graduated from Leiden, he had expressed his convictions concerning the forms of unity. In a work entitled "Voice of a Watchman on Zion's Walls" he wrote, "Earlier already I was heartily and in all points agreed with the confessions of the Reformed church."[12]

During the course of his first few months in Drogeham, Van Velzen was befriended by a certain Rev. S. Hogerzeil from the neighboring towns of Augsbuurt and Kollumerzwaag. Hogerzeil was a conservative colleague, and the two would often meet to discuss the problem of disregard for the confessions. Hogerzeil thought they should contact all the trustworthy ministers in Friesland and organize a meeting to deal with this issue. Van Velzen believed that the proper church political route was to address a protest to the higher ecclesiastical bodies. Hogerzeil reluctantly agreed.

With this conviction, Van Velzen and Hogerzeil decided to bring the matter of the confessions to a classical board. This

---

11 Van Velzen, "The Apology of the Ecclesiastical Secession in the Netherlands," 43.

12 Van Velzen, *"Stem eens wachters op Zions muren,"* 2:170.

"classical board" was not equivalent to the "classis" of traditional Reformed polity. Melis te Velde explains:

> The classical board consisted of five to seven men, mostly ministers, who formed a permanent body supervising… the consistories. This classical board could place its own concerns on the agenda. This top-down construction opened up the possibility of a supra-local hierarchy, which contradicted the principles of the original Reformed church order.[13]

The congregations that Van Velzen and Hogerzeil served resided under the Classical Board of Dokkum, which consisted of eight area ministers.[14] It was therefore to the June 1835 meeting of this board that the two protestants intended to come.

Van Velzen was destined to go alone, however. When Van Velzen and his wife—four months pregnant at the time—arrived at the Hogerzeil manse, he discovered that his colleague had gotten cold feet. No amount of persuasion could change Hogerzeil's mind: he was not going. So, while Johanna waited anxiously with the Hogerzeils, Simon made the rest of the journey by himself.

Van Velzen recorded what happened when he arrived before the Dokkum board:

> I looked for someone to read my letter because I did not want to give the impression that I was pushing myself

---

13 Melis te Velde, "The Dutch Background of the American Secession from the RCA in 1857," in *Breaches and Bridges*, 90.

14 Later correspondence between Van Velzen and the Classical Board of Dokkum show the following eight men as members of this board: Riedel, F. Bekius, P. A. C. Hugenholtz, H. F. T. Fokkens, P. Sytsema, S. van Kleppens, W. R. van der Weide, and L. D. Westerloo. Cf. Van Velzen, "*Stem eens wachters op Zions muren*," 2:197.

to the foreground, being a newcomer. But when no one volunteered I had no choice but to do it myself. I asked for silence and all conversation stopped. After I had read the letter, I asked if anyone had a comment to make. But again total silence ensued. Well, I said, silence lends consent. I ask you therefore to proceed with signing this petition. At this someone spoke up. "Not me," he said, "I won't sign." "I won't either" said another.[15]

None of his colleagues were willing to support him. At that point, one of the men suggested discussing Van Velzen's letter over their meal, a suggestion that was met with approval by the other members of the board but with surprise by Van Velzen, who could not understand why they would discuss such a serious matter over a meal.

On the way to the room where the meal was to be served, a colleague who was a total stranger to Van Velzen approached and said quietly, "What have you done? The men are very upset with you."

To which Van Velzen replied, "Do you agree with my letter?"

"Yes, I do," he said, "but none of the others do."

"Well, sign then."

"But I can't," he replied, "not in the circumstances I'm in. But I will protect you, because chances are they are going to throw you down the stairs."

When the board's meal was served, Van Velzen joined them but was relegated to a separate table. The food was exquisite, and

---

15 Many of the quotations and information regarding this incident come from Cornelis Pronk, *A Goodly Heritage: The Secession of 1834 and Its Impact on Reformed Churches in the Netherlands and North America* (Grand Rapids, MI: Reformation Heritage Books, 2019), 116–17. Some are my quotations from Van Velzen, "*Stem eens wachters op Zions muren*," 2:179.

the drink overflowed. The wine apparently loosened the tongues of the board members. Soon they were making elaborate toasts.

"To the King!" shouted one.

"To peace and love in the church!" bellowed another.

Van Velzen did not participate, a fact that was not overlooked by the others. "Why doesn't he drink with us?"

Van Velzen responded in disgust, "I find it appalling that ministers deal in such a way with the most sacred of matters."

This angered his colleagues. One overindulgent colleague, presumably half-drunk, spoke for the group when he bellowed, "I'd rather have my neck wrung than subscribe to the Canons of Dordt."[16]

The Dokkum board stormed at Van Velzen, pressing in upon him with the intention of attacking him. The colleague who had warned him came to his aid at this point, standing behind Van Velzen to defend him if necessary. They called him a sanctimonious and hypocritical Pharisee and said that he ought to be thrown out of the room.

This was the last straw for Van Velzen. He reminded them that he was only concerned about the well-being of the church. He expressed to them his forgiveness and his desire that they seek forgiveness from the Lord. Then he arose and exited the meeting.

Although he was disappointed, Van Velzen's zeal for the confessions was not quenched. Since his approach had failed, he and Hogerzeil turned now to the latter's suggestion. Together they tried to call a meeting of all orthodox ministers in the area. But

---

16 Van Velzen, *Gedenkschrift der Christelijke Gereformeerde Kerk, bij Vijftig-jarig Jubilé, 14 October 1884* [Memorial of the Christian Reformed Church, at the fifty-year anniversay, 14 October 1884] (Kampen: G. Ph. Zalsman, 1884), 90, http://www.neocalvinisme.nl/tekstframes.html (accessed July 16, 2020). Translated in David J. Engelsma, "The Covenant Doctrine of the Fathers of the Secession," in *Always Reforming*, 102.

this attempt was fruitless also. Only one other man showed up, and he was Hogerzeil's brother-in-law (Rev. G. Landweer from Birdaard). Van Velzen thought they should still meet and echoed Jesus's words in Matthew 18:20: "For where two or three are gathered together in my name, there am I in the midst of them." But the other two were dissatisfied and went home.[17]

Shortly thereafter, Van Velzen traveled to Amsterdam and Gelderland to get advice from others on how to proceed. While staying in Hattem with the Brummelkamps, he met with Isaac da Costa and a Rev. Witteveen to discuss what must be done to reform the church. Witteveen told Van Velzen, "God must do it, not us." Da Costa shrugged his shoulders: "Do nothing! Wait."[18]

But Brummelkamp's advice was different. He revealed to his brother-in-law that he was drafting a letter to the synodical board in which he called them to defend and maintain the historic Reformed creeds.

Van Velzen was motivated to do the same. He addressed a letter, dated July 6, 1835, to the Synodical Board of the Hervormde Kerk. After observing that the Reformed confessions and the doctrines contained in them were rejected and hated by many ministers, Van Velzen made three requests:

1. That our three forms of unity have a binding power for all who occupy the office of preacher in our Reformed Church, and accordingly all ministers be required to proclaim this doctrine.
2. That all ministers who reject the forms and thus despise the truth and love the lie be prevented from

---

17 The other minister was Rev. G. Landweer of Birdaard.
18 Quoted in Wagenaar, Het *"Reveil" en de "Afscheiding,"* 194–95; Van Gelderen, *Simon van Velzen,* 26.

introducing their errors in our church and seducing the congregation of the Lord.

3. That the faithful servants of the Lord who openly show their devotion to the true doctrine not be reproached or excluded by the only board in the church but be protected.[19]

Within just eight days, the synodical board evaluated and responded to Van Velzen's overture: request denied. What's more, Van Velzen and Brummelkamp were branded as "snakes."[20]

◆ ◆ ◆

The third area about which Van Velzen was troubled was the church's worship. Van Velzen's concern for proper worship is evident from his objections to the singing of hymns in public worship.

In 1807, a songbook was adopted by the churches that included 192 "evangelical hymns." "These hymns," one author writes, "were deeply influenced by the spirit of the times and spoke in a very 'enlightened' way about morals, progress, and peace and blessing for virtuous people. But there was hardly any emphasis on the doctrines of grace."[21] Not only was this hymnbook approved for use in the churches, but the synodical board later mandated that every minister include at least one of the hymns in every worship service.

Many pious souls could not in good conscience sing from this hymnbook. When a hymn was announced, some would put their hat back on as a way of indicating that they were not going to join in. Others were more brazen and walked out of the building until the hymn was over.[22]

Interestingly, this was not Van Velzen's position at first. He was initially comfortable using the hymnbook:

> As far as I was concerned, I had no problem with the hymnbook used by the Reformed Church. I believed that while psalm singing should be the norm for congregational singing, they did not have to be sung exclusively. Although I was aware that some of the hymns in the book were objectionable from a doctrinal point of view, I also knew that some of the rhymed psalms contained expressions that were also problematic. Besides, there were some hymns that spoke to my heart and therefore I thought I could announce them in good conscience. So I suggested we'd sing psalms plus some of these better hymns. However, the congregation was not to be persuaded to give up its practice of singing only psalms. So I suggested that henceforth we would sing only psalms. But what will be the result of that, they asked me? It will probably get me into trouble with the ecclesiastical authorities, I replied; they will likely remove me from office, but so be it; I will not let that keep me from doing what's right...When I said that, they would not hear of quitting hymn singing because they certainly did not want to lose their pastor.[23]

Although Van Velzen was himself comfortable using the hymnbook, he was opposed to the idea of forcing these hymns upon an unwilling congregation. Van Velzen raised the issue with

---

22 Pieters, "Historical Introduction," in *Classis Holland Minutes 1848–1858*, 11.
23 Quoted in Pronk, *A Goodly Heritage*, 118.

his consistory less than fourteen days after his ordination. The consistory's response was to continue using the hymns because they did not want their young pastor to run into problems with the ecclesiastical boards.

The issue came up again a few months later when, on June 28, 1835, Van Velzen called the congregation together to decide on whether to use hymns. The consistory minutes record, "The general feeling of the congregation was that, although desirous to have the hymns removed, nevertheless we must tolerate them as long as no one was being forced to sing them."[24]

At about that same time, Van Velzen received encouragement on the hymn question from his brothers-in-law Brummelkamp and Van Raalte. These two men and their wives came to spend several weeks of vacation in Drogeham. The men privately discussed the issues they were facing, then Brummelkamp gave a public lecture in Drogeham to address the problem of hymns. In addition, the two also preached for Van Velzen on August 16 and August 23, and neither of them announced any hymns during the worship services.

Because of Van Velzen's stance on the confessions and on hymns, he received a visit from a committee of Classis Dokkum shortly after his exchange with the synodical board. The committee wanted to discuss with him his letter to the board, his refusal to use hymns, and his permitting Brummelkamp and Van Raalte to preach in his congregation without using hymns.

Van Velzen appeared again before a full meeting of the classical board on September 30. They scolded him for saying that some ministers in the denomination hated the truth and asked him directly what he thought of the ecclesiastical boards. It was

---

24 Quoted in Van Gelderen, *Simon van Velzen*, 24.

at this meeting that Van Velzen said the boards were in direct conflict with God's word and the three forms of unity.

For this response and his other objections, Van Velzen received notice from the classical board that they were going to initiate the process of suspending him from office.[25] The Drogeham consistory minutes of October 20 record the following: "There was read a decision of the Classical Board of Dokkum whereby the minister of this congregation is suspended...This suspension must commence on November 8, 1835, and will last six weeks."[26]

During the intervening days between the reading of this decision and the implementing of his suspension, a change came over Van Velzen with respect to the hymn question. And it came, in the providence of God, in dramatic fashion.

Because people came from miles around to hear the gospel preached faithfully by Van Velzen, the church building in Drogeham was often bursting at the seams. Such was the case on Sunday, November 1. Van Velzen and his consistory decided to hold services outside in the church cemetery so as to accommodate all the visitors. When Simon was finished with his sermon, he announced that one of the required hymns would be sung. But he immediately noticed that a majority of the congregants started filing out among the tombstones in order to avoid singing a hymn. Van Velzen quickly changed course and announced that they were not going to sing the hymn but would sing a psalm instead. The congregation came streaming back into the cemetery and sang lustily the first two verses of Psalm 68.

---

25 For the classical board's decision, cf. A. Tjoelker, *Ds. S. van Velzen en zijn betekenis voor de Afscheiding in Friesland: Een kerk-hisorische bijdrage over de Jaren 1835–1840* [Rev. S. van Velzen and his significance for the Secession in Friesland: A church history contribution on the years 1835–1840] (Leeuwarden: A. Jongbloed, 1935), 108–9.

26 Quoted in Dalhuysen, *"De afscheiding van S. van Velzen,"* 270–71.

The importance of this event was driven home to Van Velzen on the very next night. On that night, Van Velzen's wife experienced the pangs of birth and was ready to deliver their first child. The doctor was summoned, and Johanna gave birth to a son, whom they named Simon after his father and grandfather. After the child was born, the doctor turned to Van Velzen and said that on the previous night he had been on call in a neighboring town lying about four miles away across the countryside. So hearty was the singing of Psalm 68, the doctor reported, that he was able to hear the voices reverberating across the fields.

From that moment, Van Velzen was convinced that he could not permit hymns any longer. On November 15, he announced to his congregation that he would only be using psalms in the worship services. And on November 17, he informed the Classical Board of Dokkum of this decision. He wrote that this decision was made not only for the peace of the congregation but also for the peace of his own soul. He felt compelled to obey God rather than men regarding hymns.

Because of his supposed insolence, Van Velzen was again summoned before the Classical Board of Dokkum. He appeared on November 25 to answer questions concerning his refusal to use the approved hymns. Van Velzen conveyed to the board his utter disgust with the fact that he was being questioned and censured for his position on hymns while other ministers were promoting the baldest of heresies without any consequences. The board's response? "Out of prudence we do not desire to speak about this."[27]

On December 10, 1835, Van Velzen received notice from Classis Dokkum that he was again suspended and that the matter

---

27 Van Velzen, *"Stem eens wachters op Zions muren,"* 2:212.

of his permanent dismissal from office was now being considered by the Provincial Board of Friesland.

At about this time, Van Velzen also received an unexpected but welcome guest at the Drogeham manse. This visitor would have an important influence on Van Velzen's next move.

Chapter 6

SECESSION

*T*he visitor to Drogeham on that cold December day was none other than Hendrik de Cock, leader of the Secession.

Although De Cock and Van Velzen had not yet established the close relationship that they would later enjoy, this was not the first meeting of these two young reformers. The two had been acquainted with each other for several months. The past August, while Van Velzen's brothers-in-law Brummelkamp and Van Raalte were staying with him, De Cock had paid them a visit. That was the first time that they had all met face-to-face. De Cock was aware of their objections to what was going on in the state church through their letters to the synodical board, and, somehow learning that the three were together, he made a point of coming to see them in order to become acquainted. What was said at that first meeting is known only to God, but shortly thereafter Brummelkamp broke with the Hervormde Kerk. De Cock likely encouraged the brothers-in-law in their struggles against the apostasy of the church.[1]

---

1   Harm Veldman, *Hendrik de Cock (1801–1842)*, 2:381. The second volume is available only on CDROM. According to Veldman, the date was August 17. Te Velde gives the date as August 18 (*Anthony Brummelkamp*, 65).

Now, in the midst of Van Velzen's struggles with the mother church, De Cock appeared in Drogeham again. The reformer had been in the province instituting new congregations, but he took time out of his busy schedule to visit with Van Velzen.[2] It was December 5, and Van Velzen's status in the church was becoming more and more precarious by the day. Later that day, De Cock reflected on their visit, "Today, with freedom of my mind, I have been with Rev. van Velzen at the church, because he has rejected the hymns. But if he does not go further, I would not do it again as the result."[3] At this meeting, De Cock probably urged Van Velzen to go beyond quarreling over hymns and make a final break with the Hervormde Kerk.

It is no coincidence that this was exactly what Van Velzen did. Five days later, as noted above, Van Velzen received notice that he was again suspended and his permanent deposition was being considered. The handwriting was on the wall; his brief career in the mother church was soon over. Knowing this, Van Velzen called a meeting of the congregation for the very next day, December 11. After opening with the singing of a psalm and prayer to God, he informed the members that he was not able to abide by the decision of the classical board and that he was seceding from the Hervormde Kerk. He was three days short of his twenty-sixth birthday.

---

2   Prior to the meeting with Van Velzen, De Cock had instituted the Frisian congregations in Sneek (November 27), Bolsward (November 27), Minnertsga (December 1), Sexbierum/Harlingen (December 1), Ferwerd (December 3), Blija (December 3), and Marrum (December 4). After their meeting, he would institute the congregation in Leeuwarden (December 8). Earlier that year he had instituted the congregation in Burum (June 21). Cf. Veldman, *Hendrik de Cock (1801–1842)*, 2:6, 8.

3   Quoted in Van Gelderen, *Simon van Velzen*, 29.

Besides Van Velzen and his wife, only eight confessing members—one man and seven women—and twenty-eight people in total were willing to secede.[4] That night, these courageous men and women signed a brief letter of secession that they addressed to the ecclesiastical boards:

> The undersigned are united in the fear and power of the Lord with the true Reformed church, and reject the Board in the *Nederlandse Hervormde Kerk* as antichristian, in accordance with article 28 of our Confession of Faith.[5]

Van Velzen added a warning: "In His name I proclaim to the Netherlands Reformed Church which persecutes the Lord Christ in His members, the wrath of Almighty God. This wrath will strike in this and in the future life, for He said: 'Touch not mine anointed, and do my prophets no harm' (Psalm 105:15)."[6]

Within a few days of this meeting, several other members cast their lot in with the seceders, bringing the total to forty-four. But this number was only a small portion of the congregation. One historian put it succinctly but accurately: "Drogeham left Van Velzen almost alone."[7] Regarding this situation, Van Velzen wrote to De Cock shortly thereafter, "The building of Zion proceeds continually in this province, although in the place where I live it goes very slowly."[8]

---

4 The one man was Sjouke Storm, and the seven women were Sjoukje Jitzes Bosma, Wietske Harmes Kijlstra, Antje Hendriks Jager, Sietske Geerts Spoelstra, Trijntje Jans van der Veen, Geertje Jeens Postma, and Antje Wiberens de Jongh. Cf. Dalhuysen, "*De afscheiding van S. van Velzen*," 264; Keizer, "*Een paar brieven van wijlen Prof. S. van Velzen*," 400n2.
5 Quoted in Van Velzen, "*Stem eens wachters op Zions muren*," 2:214.
6 Quoted in Pronk, *A Goodly Heritage*, 119.
7 Kromminga, *The Christian Reformed Tradition*, 87.
8 Quoted in Keizer, "*Een paar brieven van wijlen Prof. S. van Velzen*," 400.

Of those who seceded, none were elders or deacons, much to Van Velzen's sorrow. In a note added to the consistory's minute book, he wrote, "The elders and deacons have desired to retain the favor of the antichristian Board. Therefore, grievous afflictions from the Most High await these unfaithful men. Amen."[9] To fill the void, the newly-seceded group quickly elected two men to serve as officebearers: Roel Jans Kamminga as elder and Tamme Hendriks Uitterdijk as deacon.[10]

Once Van Velzen made this break, he received another visit from De Cock on December 14 (his birthday). Accompanying him on this occasion was Jochum Andriessen, a recently-ordained elder in the Secession church of nearby Sneek. Tradition has it that De Cock and Andriessen arrived in Drogeham on ice skates, a popular and effective means of transportation during the cold winter months, when the many canals crisscrossing the countryside were frozen solid. Although cold outside, there was warmth and excitement in the Drogeham parsonage as the three discussed the future of the Afscheiding in Friesland.[11]

The only thing that remained was for the mother church to

---

9 Quoted in Van Gelderen, *Simon van Velzen*, 28.

10 When Van Velzen was unable to preach in Drogeham, he commissioned Deacon Uitterdijk to lead the services rather than Elder Kamminga because the latter was eighty years old. When Uitterdijk was first informed of this, he objected that he had never even prayed in public before. Van Velzen assured him that the Lord would provide for him in his time of need. Uitterdijk later trained for the ministry under Hendrik de Cock and Tamme Foppes de Haan, and was installed as the pastor of the Frisian congregation in Joure on May 8, 1842. Cf. Wesseling, *De Afscheiding van 1834 in Friesland*, 2:44, 55.

11 Van Gelderen notes the tradition of using ice skates (*Simon van Velzen*, 29). However, he claims that De Cock and Andriessen "apparently" came on December 5, while Veldman makes the correction that the December 5 meeting was made by De Cock alone and the December 14 meeting by De Cock and Andriessen (*Hendrik de Cock (1801–1842)*, 2:383).

acknowledge Van Velzen's departure. They did so on January 13, 1836. The Provincial Synod of Friesland deposed Van Velzen, and then, adding insult to injury, they fined him a staggering 257 guilders for the troubles he had caused them.[12]

◆ ◆ ◆

Van Velzen's departure from the mother church brought about immediate changes, both in his ministerial labors and in his family life.

Because he no longer belonged to the denomination, he was obligated to vacate the parsonage in Drogeham. The denomination held possession of this and all other properties. It appeared as if he and his wife and their one-month-old son would be left out in the cold. But their next-door neighbor, a weaver by the name of S. D. Schivink, took pity on them. Even though this man did not agree with Van Velzen's theological convictions, he nevertheless wrote to him and expressed his desire to provide them with a place to live: "Reverend! I have a request for you and yours. If it please the Triune God to keep you in this place as pastor and teacher, even if you should have your house built in my garden, I am willing to do it for your work."[13] Van Velzen was deeply moved by the gesture: "I think his lines are worth more than gold or rubies, than a knight's mark or ribbon of order."[14]

Not only was Simon evicted from the parsonage, but he was

---

12 Van Velzen, "*Stem eens wachters op Zions muren*," 2:216–26. For the sake of comparison, some families lived on 250 guilders or less per year. A Secession minister's salary was commonly set at 500 guilders a year, but rarely did he receive it. Cf. H. Algra, *Het wonder van de 19e eeuw: Van vrije kerken en kleine luyden* [The miracle of the 19th century: of free churches and little people] (Franeker: T. Wever, 1976), 243–46.

13 Quoted in Tjoelker, *Ds. S. van Velzen*, 45.

14 Quoted in Tjoelker, *Ds. S. van Velzen*, 45.

also prevented from entering the pulpit. Upon hearing of his secession, the classical board quickly arranged for Rev. L. D. Westerloo to preach on Sunday, December 13. He was promised that nine local police officers would be present to help keep the peace.

Barred from the pulpit, Van Velzen arranged to preach that Sunday in the barn of a local dairy farmer, Cornelis Praamstra. Word spread quickly, and nearly three hundred people were present in that humble setting to hear faithful preaching of the gospel as Van Velzen led the service from atop Praamstra's wagon. The same arrangements were made on the following Sunday, with the same results. A few days later was Christmas, and Van Velzen was again found preaching in the barn. While he was reading the scriptures, two government officials entered to observe what was going on. Van Velzen led another service that day in the afternoon, but now to an audience that had ballooned to almost five hundred members, excluding the two government officials. The officials reported to their superiors about the unauthorized services, and Van Velzen was fined fifty guilders.

It was the beginning of a busy and controversial new chapter in his ministry.

◆ ◆ ◆

But was it really necessary? That was the question raised by many at the time of the Secession, a question that is still raised today.

Many in Van Velzen's day questioned whether it was necessary to go to the extreme measure of seceding from the Hervormde Kerk. They judged that although conditions were far from ideal in the mother church, things had not regressed to the point of her being a false church. In their judgment, it was improper to secede, and the proper course of action was to have worked for reform from within the institute.

Such was the attitude of many ministers in the church, including a number who had a reputation for being quite conservative. This was also the attitude of the influential men of the Reveil. Although the Reveil leaders were advocating for changes in the church and were on friendly terms with the leaders of the Secession, they strongly opposed the step of leaving the church.

This same attitude is shared by many today. In his recent book on Hendrik Scholte, Eugene Heideman does not commit himself to one position or another: "This book does not provide an answer to the question of the necessity of the Secession," he writes. While he is sympathetic to the Secession, nevertheless he is also "comfortable with the decision of professors and fellow students in Utrecht who believed that separation from the church of the land was a serious mistake."[15]

Many years after the Secession (1848), Van Velzen wrote a work defending the Secession over against the critics who claimed it was unnecessary. In his *Apology of the Ecclesiastical Secession in the Netherlands*, he argued that the Secession was necessary because the mother church was not faithful to the Reformed confessions. Van Velzen asked a series of rhetorical questions:

> Are not the creeds of the Reformed church actually abolished in the official state Reformed Church? Is not unbelief's every false doctrine tolerated and honored in its midst under the guise of biblical slogans, yes, even with disdain for the slogan? Does not the official state Reformed Church mock and reject the legal authority of the creedal documents?[16]

---

15 Heideman, *Hendrik P. Scholte*, xx.
16 This and the following quotations from Van Velzen are taken from "The Apology of the Ecclesiastical Secession in the Netherlands," 41–8.

Later he wrote, "When it must be acknowledged that unbelief dominates the ruling body of the official state Reformed Church, and that the ruling body is absolutely poisonous for the Reformed church, then whoever knows this, and nonetheless does not leave, becomes guilty as well."

Van Velzen then argued that the state church was not content merely to allow false doctrine to be taught. They also tried to silence the mouths of those who taught the truth and condemned the lie.

> Not only did the ruling body honor the deniers of the confession, but they also persecuted those who defended the creeds. Why did the ruling body of the official Reformed Church suspend and depose the shepherd and preacher H. De Cock, with others, among whom I am also numbered? They did this only because we confronted those who opposed the faith and because we came out candidly for the truth and the rights of the church.

Van Velzen and his comrades "were deposed, while the churches continued to be entrusted to public opponents of the faith of the Reformed church, to mockers of the creeds, and to those who denied the truth."

Van Velzen further argued that the leaders of the Secession did not walk away from the church quickly and thoughtlessly. The seceding ministers had carried out the work of reformation in the right manner. The moment they became convinced of the errors of the church, they did not immediately walk out. They tried to follow the proper channels to show the church her errors and bring about reformation from within. "We did not leave the state Reformed Church arbitrarily. We did not forsake our appointed posts. If I had not been hindered in laboring faithfully,

I would have gladly and thankfully remained in my relationship to the congregation of Drogeham." Van Velzen did all he could to show the assemblies that they were walking contrary to God's word and the Reformed confessions. As a good watchman, he called the church to return to the biblical pattern set out for her.

Only when it became plain that the church refused to allow reform did Van Velzen leave and reform the church by forming a new church institute. In fact, in Van Velzen's estimate, it was the church that had put him out, and not he who had walked away. "The superior authority of the governing body of the church evicted me." Van Velzen was aware that he had seceded from the church prior to his official deposition, but it was clear that the church was going to expel him. He had done all he could from within the church body. Faithfulness to God now meant leaving the corrupt mother church and forming a new institute.

For these reasons, Van Velzen was convinced that the state church had become a false church. "It all comes down to this: that the Netherlands Reformed (*Hervormde*) Church is not the true, but the false church, according to God's Word and Article 29 of the Belgic Confession of Faith." One of the marks of the false church, according to this article, is that she "persecutes those who live holily according to the word of God, and rebuke her for her errors, covetousness, and idolatry."[17] This was certainly true of the state church when she disciplined Van Velzen and persecuted him and the other reformers.

The necessity of the Secession can hardly be questioned. Van Velzen and the other leaders had tried to bring about reformation from within the denomination. They had protested the errors that they saw in the church. They had tried to lead the church

---

17 *The Confessions and Church Order of the Protestant Reformed Churches* (Grandville, MI: Protestant Reformed Churches in America, 2005), 64.

back to the standard of God's word and the Reformed confessions. But the mother church refused to follow their leading and instead began the process of removing them from office. Van Velzen and the others were left with two choices: be removed from office and continue as members in an unfaithful denomination, or leave and reform the church by forming a new institute. They could not do the former with a good conscience before God. The only alternative left to them was secession and the forming of a new denomination that was more faithful to God's word and the Reformed confessions.

In another place, Van Velzen wrote regarding seceding, "With my hand on my heart, I may not, I cannot do otherwise!"[18]

---

18 Van Velzen, "*Stem eens wachters op Zions muren*," 2:253.

PART 3

CHURCHMAN

(1836–54)

Chapter 7

———⟶ ❖ ⟵———

EARLY YEARS OF THE AFSCHEIDING

The Secession was a true reformation, a wonderful work of God in preserving and reforming his church. For that reason, the seceders could rejoice in the work of forming a new denomination that was faithful to the word of God and the Reformed confessions. But, with the excitement came a deep sense of responsibility. For Van Velzen and the others, it meant doing mountains of work while enduring never-ending hardship and persecution.

By seceding from the mother church, Van Velzen and the Drogeham faithful joined a small, despised group of fellow seceders. For the most part, the seceders did not belong to the social elite. The wealthy landowners and "enlightened" aristocracy looked down their noses at the movement. Many seceders belonged to the middle class; they were either small tradesmen or poorer farmers. A significant number also belonged to the "upper-lower" class. They were mostly hired hands who possessed no land and little money, but yet were not totally destitute. Official government reports at the time of the Secession described the seceders as "for the most part…from the lowest ranks." They were "uncultured," "the least significant," having "no man of name" among them.[1]

Although small in comparison to the bloated numbers of the mother church, the new denomination experienced tremendous growth in the early years. Flocks of people left the Hervormde Kerk, and seceder congregations began to pop up all over the country. Exact numbers are impossible to find, but by the end of 1835 there were about 20,000 souls distributed among 80 congregations,[2] and by the end of 1836 there were in the neighborhood of 130 congregations.[3]

The reality of a fledgling denomination with ballooning numbers meant ceaseless labor for the small band of ministers that served her. There were only six of them. Besides Van Velzen, De Cock, and Scholte, the only other Secession ministers in those early days were Anthony Brummelkamp, George Frans Gezelle Meerburg, and Johannes van Rhee. Brummelkamp seceded on November 21, 1835, and the other two seceded on November 24. These men were all relatively young and inexperienced. With

---

1   Bratt, *Dutch Calvinism in Modern America*, 6, 226n16.
2   Hommo Reenders, "Albertus C. van Raalte: The *Homo Oecumenicus* among the Secession Leaders," *Calvin Theological Journal* 33, no. 2 (November 1998): 278.
3   Bratt says that at an early stage there were 128 congregations (*Dutch Calvinism in Modern America*, 7). Another source suggests that there were 137 congregations. Cf. Martijn de Groot, "Geruisloze verandering: Onderzoek naar de identiteitsontwikkeling van de Gereformeerde Kerken in Nederland na de Vrijmaking (1944–1961)" ["Silent change: examination of the development of the identity of the Reformed Churches in the Netherlands after the Liberation (1944–1961)"] (master's thesis, Theologische Universiteit Apeldoorn, 2010), 8, https://hdc.vu.nl/nl/Images/groot.Masterscriptie_Geruisloze_verandering_tcm215-169525.pdf (accessed November 26, 2012). Another source says that by the end of 1839 there were about 150 congregations (Algra, *Het wonder van de 19e eeuw*, 100).

the exception of De Cock and Van Rhee, none were yet even thirty years old.

◆ ◆ ◆

The first few months of Van Velzen's time as a "father" of the Secession were a whirlwind of emotion and activity for the young pastor. The demands upon him and his fellow ministers required that they work long hours. One of his colleagues confessed that he often worked until four o'clock in the morning.

Van Velzen faced many of the same struggles as his fellow Secession ministers. For one thing, he was essentially responsible for the spiritual care of an entire province. Because of the growing number of churches and the extreme shortage of ministers at this early stage of the reformation, each minister became responsible for all the Secession churches in a particular province. De Cock labored primarily in the province of Groningen, Scholte worked among the people of North and South Holland, Brummelkamp was assigned the province of Gelderland, and Gezelle Meerburg and Van Rhee had North Brabant. Likewise, Van Velzen was asked to tend to the needs of the churches in the province of Friesland.

Prior to Van Velzen's secession, De Cock had traveled through Friesland on a kind of "missionary journey," during which he instituted a number of Secession churches.[4] On January 1, 1836, delegates from these churches met in the capital city of Leeuwarden.[5] They convened the first Provincial Synod of Friesland and

---

4   Veldman, *Hendrik de Cock (1801–1842)*, 2:380–83.
5   The delegates were: A. J. Veenstra (deacon from Marrum), T. H. Uitterdijk (deacon from Drogeham), M. S. Millema (elder from Blija), M. A. IJpma (deacon from Minnertsga), J. Meijering (deacon from Leeuwarden), K. Hogendijk (elder from Ferwerd), Jurjen R. Haitsma (elder from Harlingen), Gerben E. Folkertsma (elder from Boornbergum), W. A. van der Heide (deacon from Bolswaard), R. D. Hamming (elder from Burum), and A. G. Bakker (deacon from Sneek). Cf. Tjoelker, *Ds. S. van Velzen*, 48.

unanimously called Van Velzen to be pastor and teacher for the entire province. They promised to pay him 850 guilders a year in addition to providing free housing. Van Velzen readily accepted the call.

Since his deposition from the Hervormde Kerk meant he had to vacate the Drogeham parsonage and since the care of the churches in Friesland was not something he could carry out effectively from the small village of Drogeham, Van Velzen planned to relocate his family to Leeuwarden and make that city his base of operations.

Meanwhile, Van Velzen was kept busy with the needs of the Frisian churches. His work involved constant travel through the countryside in order to preach the gospel, administer the sacraments, lead consistory meetings, and organize new congregations. On January 6, for instance, he instituted a combined congregation from the towns of Wanswerd and Birdaard with five confessing members.[6] Later that month, he wrote to De Cock and reported on his extensive travel plans. "This coming Saturday," he wrote, "I intend to go and visit the secession churches in Sneek and Bolswaard, and thereafter to travel through Harlingen and other places to Heerenveen while I institute some churches along the way."[7]

After a rigorous two months, Van Velzen finally found time to move his family to Leeuwarden on Saturday, February 27, with the help of Elder J. Meijering from Leeuwarden and Deacon T. H. Uitterdijk from Drogeham. But, he had no time to settle in. They had just arrived at the doorstep of their new home when they were met by Pier Ottes de Jong. De Jong was a resident of the

---

6   Wesseling, *De Afscheiding van 1834 in Friesland*, 1:157. The leader of this group was an elder named Pieter Symens van der Woude, who led the services when a minister was not available and who was frequently delegated to synod.

7   Van Velzen to De Cock, January 27, 1836, in Keizer, "*Een paar brieven van wijlen Prof. S. van Velzen*," 400–1.

neighboring town of Wolvega and insisted that Van Velzen come immediately and institute a church there. Van Velzen agreed. He and his wife dropped off their belongings at their new home and left straight away with De Jong for Wolvega. That night, between forty and fifty men and women from Wolvega and neighboring communities gathered silently in a barn belonging to one of the members. They dared not open their mouths to sing because of the intense persecution they were facing. Van Velzen preached for them and then instituted the new congregation with De Jong as one of the first elders.

Still, he had no time to rest. By early Monday morning, Van Velzen and his wife were on their way again, traveling south to Hattem to visit the Brummelkamps. The first synod of the Secession was to be held later that week, and Van Velzen and Brummelkamp were both required to attend. After leaving his wife with her sister, Van Velzen and his brother-in-law continued on to Amsterdam, where synod was held in a warehouse owned by the mother-in-law of Scholte.

It comes as no surprise that the minutes of the synod indicate Van Velzen was sick. This sickness was likely induced by stress and exhaustion. Perhaps he had reached the point of a break-down. In the last few months, he had experienced a number of life-changing events: his first child was born; he seceded from the Hervormde Kerk; he traveled extensively while preaching, instituting new congregations, and giving advice to consistories; he endured persecution; he uprooted his family and moved to a new home; and then he still had to make it to Amsterdam on time for synod.[8] And for Van Velzen and the other synodical

---

8   He and Brummelkamp still did not make it to synod on time; they entered the meeting shortly after it had opened. Cf. article 5, *Handelingen en versla-gen van de Algemene synoden van de Christelijik Afgescheidene Gereformeerde*

delegates, there was the added pressure of the difficult synodical agenda as well as the fear of harassment by the civil authorities. "That synod," one man recalled, "was held in a warehouse on the Baangracht. Because of the possibility of persecution, it had to meet without any fanfare and in a place which the police would not easily be able to find."[9] Nevertheless, there was work to be done, and Van Velzen refused to slow down.

◆ ◆ ◆

Building where first synod was held

A predominant concern of that first synod was the severe shortage of ministers in the burgeoning denomination. Some proposed

Kerk (1836–1869) met stukken betreffende de synode van 1843, bijlagen en registers [Acts and reports of the General Synods of the Christian Secession Reformed Church (1836–1869) with documents concerning the synod of 1843, appendices, and registers] (Houten: Den Hertog, 1984), 25.

9   Quoted in Bouma, *Secession, Doleantie, and Union*, 209.

that this shortage be alleviated by ordaining *oefenaars*, the exhorters from the conventicles. But with Van Velzen leading the way,
this proposal was rejected.[10] This would spell trouble for him
later, because one congregation in Friesland so supported the use
of oefenaars that they no longer could bear to have Van Velzen
preach for them.

The need for ministers was partially met at synod by the coming of Albertus van Raalte. Van Raalte had been denied entrance
into the Hervormde Kerk because of his known connections to
the leaders of the Secession. After constituting itself, Synod 1836
immediately turned to the examination of Van Raalte. He passed
the examination, and he was shortly thereafter ordained and
installed as minister of the church of Genemuiden and Mastenbroek, although he served the entire province of Overijssel.

At the same time the churches gained one minister, they lost
another, and in scandalous fashion. Rev. Johannes van Rhee was
brought before the synod on suspicions of homosexual activity.
Suspicions had surrounded Van Rhee already from his days in
seminary. At synod, Van Rhee's case was placed into the hands
of a committee consisting of Van Velzen, De Cock, and Elder
D. Hoksbergen. After studying the case, the committee advised
synod to proceed with the deposition of Van Rhee, which advice
synod took as its own decision.[11]

In addition to addressing the need for ministers, the primary task before the synod was the matter of official government

---

10 Van Velzen's opposition to oefenaars will be explained in more detail in
    chapter 11.
11 Cf. articles 25–27, 55, 74–75, *Handelingen en verslagen*, 32–33, 46, 58–
    66. J. van Gelderen notes that Van Rhee was suspected of homosexuality
    already during his time as a student at Leiden. Cf. *Biografisch lexicon*, s.v.
    "Rhee, Johannes Van."

recognition. The synod addressed a letter to King William asking him to recognize their churches as a legitimate Reformed denomination, in distinction from the Hervormde Kerk. If the king granted this recognition, the churches of the Secession would be free from persecution. Once the letter was drafted, Rev. Brummelkamp and Elders H. G. Klijn and V. Koningsberger were delegated to bring this letter to the king. When they approached William, however, he immediately denied their request.

◆ ◆ ◆

Once synod was over, Van Velzen went back to Hattem, picked up his wife and son, and began the trip back to their new home in Leeuwarden. But in order to get home, they had to get through an angry mob who despised them for being seceders. Van Velzen recounted the incident:

> My wife with our child in her arms climbed into the wagon that stood in a place next to our dwelling. Now a wild uproar was heard. Stones, mud, clay were thrown over the fence; I saw my wife falter; the head and the clothes of our little son defiled with sludge. Then I realized the danger to my wife and child. Go back! I called… As soon as we were in the house again the windows were smashed; the uproar was increased. I sent someone to the head of the commune…to ask for protection…The police took positions in front of the house and we were safe during the night. The next day we went to Wolvega… As soon as we had ridden off after the noon meal…the people came into action. The shouting and casting things at the horse became so serious, that our waggoneer, completely confused, I thought, could no longer manage the

horse, but we got out of the place safely. Now, however, my wife was so terrified that she had to leave the vehicle to calm herself.[12]

Van Velzen's wife, Johanna, suffered greatly during those early years. Not only did she experience persecution herself, but she also struggled to see her beloved husband under such heavy abuse. This stress apparently aggravated the tuberculosis she had contracted earlier. When asked about her many years later, Van Velzen reflected, "I had a young wife, whom I loved and about whom I raved. She was suffering consumption [i.e., tuberculosis]. And when I was again in danger and she heard of it, then blood appeared again. I suffered a lot."[13]

On May 25, 1837, the faithful, God-fearing Johanna van Velzen died of tuberculosis after only three years of marriage. She died, however, in the full assurance of faith. Her last words, recorded by her husband, were: "I believe in Him who justifies the ungodly and also me. I hear the Hallelujah of the angels."[14]

A few days later, Van Velzen laid the body of his beloved wife to rest in Leeuwarden. What sorrow must have filled his heart as he stood next to her grave with their one-and-a-half-year-old son! The deep grief of a young widower and of a motherless child!

◆ ◆ ◆

After the Synod of 1836, Van Velzen's frenetic pace of work continued. What follows is a small sampling of his activity at that

---

12 Quoted in Bruins, *Albertus and Christina*, 208–9. Cf. Wormser, *Karakter en genade*, 38–39.

13 Van Velzen reportedly spoke these words to Lutzen H. Wagenaar, who recorded them in his *Het "Reveil" en de "Afscheiding*," 281.

14 Van Velzen, *"Episode uit den tijd der Kerkelijke Afscheiding in 1836*," in *Avondstemmen*, 141.

time, a sampling that is representative of the busyness of life throughout those early years in Friesland:

April 21, 1836 (Thurs.)—Presided at a consistory meeting in Sneek, where a major controversy was brewing between two elders.

April 23, 1836 (Sat.)—Presided at another consistory meeting in Sneek.

May 18, 1836 (Wed.)—Preached in Bolsward and baptized two children.

May 26, 1836 (Thurs.)—Visited the church in Wanswerd.

May 27, 1836 (Fri.)— Visited the church in Blija and Ferwerd.

May 28, 1836 (Sat.)—Visited the church in Marrum.

May 29, 1836 (Sun.)—Preached for the church in Marrum in a barn, with over five hundred people in attendance.

June 1, 1836 (Wed.)—Preached and administered the sacrament of baptism in a home in Rottum.

June 4, 1836 (Sat.)—Presided at a consistory meeting in Wolvega. Later in the day preached and administered the sacrament of baptism again in Rottum.

June 27, 1836 (Mon.)—Visited the church in Minnertsga.

July 5–8, 1836—Attended a gathering of ministers in Zwolle to address issues related to baptism.

◆ ◆ ◆

In addition to the busyness of his work and the heart-wrenching loss of his wife, Van Velzen also felt the sting of persecution. King William and the Dutch government went to great extremes to squash the Secession in those early years. The government attempted to justify their actions against the seceders by dredging up an old law from the code of Napoleon. This Article 291 stated,

> No association of more than 20 persons, whose aim is to convene daily or on certain days in order to be engaged in matters of religion, literature, politics, or other subjects, may be organized except by approbation of the High Government and under such conditions as the public authority will impose upon the association. Those who live in the house where the association congregates shall not be included in the number of persons meant in this article.[15]

The government applied this statute to the meetings of the seceders. Any worship service where more than twenty people were present was deemed illegal.

Local officials were empowered by the government to break up any such meetings that they uncovered. Additionally, the government would often billet soldiers in the homes of known seceders to prevent them from gathering in worship on the Sabbath. Besides having to foot the bill for the support of these soldiers, the seceders also had to deal with the ungodly lifestyle that these men brought into their homes. Those who were caught at an "illegal" meeting were forced to pay stiff fines. Those who housed these services were fined one hundred guilders. The ministers who conducted the services were fined the same amount,

---

15 Cited in tenZythoff, *Sources of Secession*, 49. Articles 292 and 294 added that those who were guilty of leading these associations or of housing them would be fined between sixteen and two hundred guilders.

while the elders were fined fifty guilders. Some ministers were forced to pay more than forty thousand guilders by the time the persecution ended.[16] In Friesland, the seceders paid more than 6,800 guilders to the government in the first half of 1837 alone.[17] If someone was not able to pay, either his home and property were seized and auctioned off on a Sunday or he was imprisoned.

From 1836 to 1838, many of the worship services that Van Velzen led were broken up by the authorities, and he was forced to pay a number of exorbitant fines.

At times, the government resorted even to imprisoning the seceders. Scholte was imprisoned once for five days before being released on bail. De Cock was imprisoned for a period of three months.

Persecution at Ulrum

Besides the official persecution carried out by the Dutch government, Van Velzen and his fellow seceders faced unofficial persecution at the hands of their fellow citizens, most of whom were members of the Hervormde Kerk. The seceders were treated as pariahs, mocked and ridiculed, spit at and pelted with mud and stones, and interrupted in the midst of their worship of God. On one occasion, while Van Velzen was preaching

---

16 Robert P. Swierenga, "1834 and 1857—Church Secessions and the Dutch Emigration," http://www.swierenga.com/Grafscap_pap.html (accessed September 11, 2013).

17 Keizer, "*Een paar brieven van wijlen Prof. S. van Velzen*," 401n2.

in Rotterdam, an angry mob smashed all the windows in the building in which the service was held, terrifying those who were gathered.

Of great significance were the financial ramifications of such persecution at the hands of their fellow citizens. Men who joined the reformation were fired by their employers and blackballed from getting other jobs elsewhere. Shopkeepers who attended seceder services on Sunday found that on Monday their stores were empty and regular customers gone. This brought great financial hardships upon those who were already quite poor.

With all this persecution, the seceders often gathered for worship in secret. Ministers came and went under the cover of darkness. No wonder the elders of the Afscheiding instituted the practice of meeting together to pray for safety and God's blessing before their worship services!

So desperate was one of the churches in Friesland to worship God without fear of interruption that they asked Van Velzen to lead a service at 4:00 a.m.[18] Van Velzen graciously consented and preached to a presumably drowsier crowd than usual.

One minister described the difficulty of being persecuted as being expelled from the circle of "honorable citizens" and instead being "a vagabond, outlawed, a hunted partridge on the mountains."[19]

The following anecdote testifies to the persecution that Van Velzen endured on a regular basis. On Saturday, September 17, 1836, a wagon pulled into Van Velzen's yard, and an elder from the church in Tjalleberd knocked on his door. The elder said that they desperately needed him to preach twice the next day,

---

18 The request was made by the church in Ferwerd. Cf. Veldman, *Hendrik de Cock (1801–1842)*, 2:230–31.

19 Van Raalte, quoted in Reenders, "Van Raalte," 285.

as well as baptize a baby, administer the Lord's supper, install a deacon, and solemnize a wedding. Despite the fact that his wife was desperately sick, Van Velzen felt compelled to go. The following morning, Van Velzen stood before a crowd of between four and five hundred people. After he had offered prayer to God, he opened his eyes to see a government official standing up to interrupt the service, declaring that the gathering was illegal on the basis of the Napoleonic code. The soldiers he brought with him used their rifles and bayonets to force the congregation to leave, while members of the Hervormde Kerk who had just gotten out of church looked on with amusement.

Van Velzen proceeded to assemble some of the members at another house; he attempted to administer the Lord's supper but was unable to do so because there was no bread or wine to be found. He then called for the parents whose babies needed to be baptized. Once the sacrament had been administered, word reached them that the government officials were on their way to break up this meeting. The group quickly fled to another house, where Van Velzen installed a man into the office of deacon. Immediately after the installation was completed, they were again informed that the officials were hot on their tail. They promptly gathered in a different house, where Van Velzen confirmed the marriage of a young couple. Immediately after the service was over, the soldiers appeared again and drove the people away with shouting and cursing.

That night, Van Velzen was supposed to lodge with the newly installed deacon, but when he arrived at the man's home, he found that a sergeant and four of his soldiers were being quartered there. While talking with the soldiers, Van Velzen became suspicious that they were plotting to harm him. The lady of the house whispered to him that she had heard they were going to try to kill him. Sure enough, later that night a crowd of people gathered around the house. They smashed in the windows with bricks, and the soldiers attempted to use the ensuing chaos to harm Van Velzen. But the local official came at that moment and ordered the soldiers to stand down. After a sleepless night, Van Velzen was put on a wagon by the soldiers and brought outside the village. As Van Velzen stepped out of the wagon, one of the soldiers pressed the sharp point of his bayonet into Van Velzen's back as he began to make his way home.

The persecution that Van Velzen and others experienced continued for many years. By 1840, with William II replacing his father as king, the intensity of the oppression lessened considerably. However, scattered persecution continued, with a few seceders still being brought to court and paying fines as late as 1846.

What accounts for this fierce persecution at the hands of the government and the Hervormde Kerk? Dutch historian Melis te Velde gives three main reasons. First, the Dutch government at that time had a great fear of civil unrest. They were shaken by the Belgian revolt a few years earlier and were not about to let another revolt take place. Second, many viewed the king as supreme not only in the civil sphere but also in the ecclesiastical. To this, the seceders steadfastly objected. Third, the civil authorities were largely sympathetic to the mother church and saw the Secession as an unauthorized rebellion.[20]

Te Velde fails to consider another, more basic reason for the persecution: hatred for Christ, the church, and the truth. With almost no exceptions, the leaders of the Secession believed that the Hervormde Kerk was a false church as described in the Belgic

---

20 Te Velde, *Anthony Brummelkamp*, 109–10.

Confession, article 29. While a true church loves Christ and the truth, a false church hates Christ and his word. Article 29 says:

> As for the false church, she ascribes more power and authority to herself and her ordinances than to the Word of God, and will not submit herself to the yoke of Christ …she relieth more upon men than upon Christ; and persecutes those who live holily according to the Word of God, and rebuke her for her errors, covetousness, and idolatry.[21]

Despite this persecution, the church grew by leaps and bounds. The more they were persecuted, the more others came to see the wickedness that reigned in the mother church and the need to come out from among her and be separate. It was fairly common for groups of five hundred people or more to be in attendance when Van Velzen was preaching, so great was the interest in reformation.[22] By the end of 1836, more than one hundred congregations had been instituted in the new denomination.

Tertullian's ancient maxim rings true: "The oftener we are mown down by you, the more in number we grow; the blood of Christians is seed."[23]

---

21 *Confessions and Church Order*, 64.

22 Cf. Wesseling, *De Afscheiding van 1834 in Friesland*, 1:89, for one example in Marrum.

23 Tertullian, *Apology*, vol. 3, *The Ante-Nicene Fathers*, eds. Alexander Roberts and James Donaldson (Grand Rapids, MI: William B. Eerdmans Publishing Co., 1986), 55.

Chapter 8

THE CRISIS
OF YOUTH

O ften when we look back on an event, the distance from that
   event provides a clearer perspective on what has happened.
But, it can also happen that as time passes we have historical
amnesia and forget the way things actually were. This is often the
case with the Secession. We have in our minds that after a heroic
break from an apostatizing church, God's saints lived together
happily ever after. Such was not the case.

   During the first years of the Secession, Van Velzen and his fellow ministers had more than external persecution by the Dutch
government and the Hervormde Kerk with which to cope. The
young denomination was also racked by a series of bitter internal
conflicts that fractured the fledgling denomination into a number
of splinter groups. One historian of the Secession has memorably
referred to this history as *de crisis der jeugd*—the crisis of youth.[1]
He ascribes these troubles not only to the growing pains of the
young denomination but also to the youthful zeal of the leaders. Van Velzen himself acknowledged in one place that "in the

1   Bouwman, *De crisis der jeugd.*

heat of battle, in the glow of indignation, in the zeal of youth, words escaped the pen which bear too much evidence of haste and excitement."[2]

Three main divisions took place after the initial separation. The first division happened when a number of ultra-conservative churches departed and formed the *Gereformeerde Kerken onder het Kruis* (Reformed Churches under the Cross). The second division involved a dispute between Van Velzen and his colleague H. P. Scholte, ending in Scholte's deposition and departure from the denomination. The third division occurred when Brummelkamp and a number of churches loyal to him isolated themselves from Van Velzen and the main stream of the Secession churches.[3]

Part of the reason for these disputes was the fact that the members of the Secession churches were not a homogeneous group. Individuals and groups left the mother church for many different reasons. They were united in a common cause against the Hervormde Kerk and her corruptions, but it soon became evident that the seceders were not in complete agreement with one another on all matters of doctrine and practice. There is a bit of doggerel that says, "The enemy of my enemy is my friend." In a sense, this was what happened at the time of the Secession.

---

2   Van Velzen, "*Stem eens wachters op Zions muren,*" 2:251–52.

3   Cf. C. Veenhof, *Prediking en uitverkiezing: Kort overzicht van de strijd, gevoerd in de Christelijk Afgescheidene Gereformeerde Kerk tusschen 1850 en 1870, over de plaats van de leer der uitverkiezing in de prediking* [Preaching and election: Brief overview of the struggle fought in the Christian Secession Reformed Church between 1850 and 1870 over the place of the doctrine of election in preaching] (Kampen: J. H. Kok, 1959), 7–8. Veenhof mentions five divisions; in addition to the three I have cited, he also lists the departure of Rev. H. Budding in 1839 and Rev. L. G. C. Ledeboer around 1840. These two left as individuals, and the divisions were not of the magnitude that the other three were. Therefore, for my purposes here, I chose not to include them.

Groups that were not in agreement with each other joined in common cause against a common opponent. But once free from the opponent, they came to realize that they were not on good terms with each other.

The divisions that agitated the young denomination revealed four divergent streams of thought that had been united under the Secession.[4]

First, there was the "Far Right," a stream that flowed out of the *Nadere Reformatie* (the Dutch Further Reformation of the seventeenth and eighteenth centuries which allegedly extended the reformation beyond doctrine to life and experience) and the conventicles where the *oude schrijvers* were cherished. This group was characterized by a strong conservatism, but many leaned in the direction of experientialism and subjectivism.

The second stream, which I call the "Center-Right" party, consisted of those who were raised in the Hervormde Kerk and were staunchly orthodox and confessional. Van Velzen fits in this camp.

The third stream, the "Center-Left," was also made up of those who were raised in the Hervormde Kerk and left her. This group was not as conservative and orthodox as the previous one and was willing to make concessions to the mother church. Leaders in this group were Brummelkamp and Van Raalte.

The fourth stream was unique; it essentially consisted of Hendrik Scholte and those who followed his eccentric line of thinking. They made up the "Far Left" party in the churches.

These Secession-era divisions may help us understand present-day divisions among churches in the Dutch Reformed tradition. Those who belonged to the "Far Right" party were the spiritual

---

4   Cf. Te Velde, *Anthony Brummelkamp*, 101, and *Breaches and Bridges*, 85. Both sources identify three streams of thought, rather than the four that I propose.

ancestors of the Netherlands Reformed Congregations in the Netherlands and in America, and by extension the Heritage Reformed Congregations. The divisions between the "Center-Right" and "Center-Left" parties appeared in the disagreements among the immigrants to Holland, Michigan, under Van Raalte, ending in the eventual formation of the Christian Reformed Church (CRC) in North America. The early founders of the CRC were men influenced strongly by Van Velzen, while Van Raalte and his followers were content to remain within the Reformed Church. It is possible that these divisions also played a part in the formation of the Protestant Reformed Churches in America. The founders of the PRCA were men who held to the same convictions as Van Velzen and the "Center-Right" party, while the leaders of the CRC at the time were teaching some of the same things as the leaders of the "Center-Left" party. It is impossible to understand the modern Reformed landscape without an understanding of the crisis of youth in the churches of the Reformation.

◆ ◆ ◆

The first break in the churches of the Afscheiding manifested itself already in 1837, just a few short years after the reformation began. This division stemmed from a doctrinal dispute between two of the founding fathers of the denomination: Hendrik de Cock and Hendrik Scholte. Although these two were the first to secede from the Hervormde Kerk and were the natural leaders of the movement, it soon became apparent that they had quite different views of what that reformation ought to look like.

Essentially, their differences boiled down to opposing views of ecclesiology: that is, the doctrine of the church. In particular, De Cock and Scholte had differing views of baptism, church membership, and church government.

Under the influence of the Dutch Further Reformation, which in turn was strongly influenced by the English Puritans, many seceders distinguished between a historical faith (confessing the doctrines of the church) and a saving faith (confessing that these truths apply to one personally). The result was the presence of two kinds of members in the church: those who confessed the truth but lacked the assurance of faith so that they could not in good conscience partake of the Lord's supper, and those who made full confession of their faith in Christ and were able to come to the table of the Lord. The problems arose with those who were not full members. What was their status in the church? Could they have their children baptized as covenantal children if they were not confessing members?

De Cock and Scholte clashed over this issue. Scholte opposed a broad baptism practice and held to the position that non-confessing members might not have their children baptized. De Cock thought Scholte was too idealistic and radical. He believed that the churches ought to baptize the children of those who did not feel able to make a confession of personal faith in Christ. The two men cordially discussed these differences already in May 1836, but by the middle of 1837 they were sharply divided over the issue, with both attempting to win support in the churches for their respective positions.

Their differences over church polity also stemmed from that early period. At the Synod of 1836, the churches had decided provisionally to make use of the historic Church Order of Dordt (DKO).[5] De Cock was in full agreement with this decision. But, Scholte had reservations about using this church order. His reservations were due in part to his independent streak and his

---

5   Cf. article 28, *Handelingen en verslagen*, 33–34.

firm opposition to the authority of the broader assemblies. His vision was to have a simple church order that was drawn directly from the scriptures and allowed for greater freedom. Already in December 1835, he had begun work on revising the church order to suit his eye. By August 1836, he had abandoned the denominationally-approved church order and was adhering to his own order. In July and August of 1837, Scholte presented his revised church order to the provincial synods of Utrecht, South Holland, Gelderland, and North Brabant. These gatherings did not give wholesale approval to his revision, but they were in favor of certain changes being made to the church order.

The conflicts over baptism and church order divided the churches. There was even division over how to remedy the situation. Many thought a synod ought to be called to rectify the situation, while others felt that the idea of calling a synod was premature and that things could be resolved on the local level.

In response to these problems, Van Velzen, along with his colleagues Brummelkamp and Van Raalte, initiated a special day of prayer in the churches. This indicates the seriousness of the situation. These special days of prayer were not called over light and trivial matters, but only in circumstances of great distress—such as wars, pestilence, or (as in this case) deep internal strife. On September 20, 1837, the denomination observed this day of prayer. Throughout the land, the various congregations gathered humbly to beseech God to guide them over these turbulent waters.

Shortly after this day of prayer was held, the churches called a synod to address and hopefully resolve these knotty theological questions. It had become plain that these issues were not going to go away on their own. From September 28 to October 11, 1837, synod met in the city of Utrecht. Van Velzen was chosen by the delegates to serve as president, an indication of the confidence they had in him and his ability to guide the synod through the weighty matters on the agenda.

The tension in the meeting room was heightened by the threat of persecution that constantly hung over the heads of the delegates. Van Velzen later gave this description of the circumstances under which the synod was held:

> It was then in the heat of the persecution. Night and day there stood before the entrance of the building in which the meeting was held a sentinel with his gun…The whole time during which the Synod was held, fourteen days, the delegates had to stay with each other in order that they might not be turned back by the sentinel if they went outside the building and were not allowed to reenter. They ate, drank, and slept together in the same quarters, and, not only in the meetings, but when they awoke and when they went to sleep they prayed with each other, and then always kneeling. And yet in this Synod reigned great difference of opinion to the very end.[6]

The spirit that prevailed at this synod was also captured by Albertus van Raalte in a letter to his wife. Writing "in haste in a dark corner while the disputation [was] going on," Van Raalte said:

> Now something about the meeting: Van Velzen was chosen as chairman and Scholte as clerk. Up to the present time there has been no discussion of the main issues. The different points of view which come to expression are numerous and are expressed frequently. I cannot disguise the fact that the difficulties often make me depressed. I feel the Lord alone can guard, protect and build the churches.

6   Van Velzen, *Gedenkschrift der Christelijke Gereformeerde Kerk*, 113–14.

In the eyes of people this is mysterious! Very mysterious indeed! O that the Lord would propitiate the sins of his people for sin is the cause of the great fractures in Zion.[7]

In a later letter to his wife, Van Raalte added:

When I regard things from God's point of view, now and then I enjoy relief. He does not deal with his people according to their sins. When, however, I observe desecrating disorder flowing into the church out of blindness, distrust and pride, then I become fearful…The distrust and misunderstanding…have not been taken away. If something good emerges from this meeting that will be the result of the Lord's action.[8]

Synod's first order of business was the adoption of a church order. Many, including De Cock, were in favor of adopting the DKO without any changes. Scholte, however, pushed for the adoption of his revised church order. Eventually, an entirely new church order was adopted by the synod. This church order, which later became known as the Church Order of Utrecht, consisted of one hundred articles, rather than the eighty-six of the DKO.[9]

---

7   Van Raalte to Christina Johanna Van Raalte-De Moen, Utrecht, October 2, 1837, in *From Heart to Heart*, 15–16. Van Raalte also mentioned in the letter that "Bro. Van Velzen does not have time to write." For alternate translations, cf. Hyma, *Van Raalte*, 38–39; Reenders, "Van Raalte," 283.

8   Van Raalte to Christina Johanna Van Raalte-De Moen, Utrecht, October 4, 1837, in *From Heart to Heart*, 19.

9   Te Velde, *Anthony Brummelkamp*, 96–97. Cf. also Oostendorp, *H. P. Scholte*, 110–14; Janet Sjaarda Sheeres, *Son of Secession: Douwe J. Vander Werp,* The Historical Series of the Reformed Church in America 52 (Grand Rapids, MI: William B. Eerdmans Publishing Co., 2006), 58–59; Ronald L. Cammenga, "The Secession of 1834 and the Struggle for the Church Order of Dordt," in *Always Reforming*, 93–99. For the text of the Church Order of Utrecht, cf. *Handelingen en verslagen*, 1122–57.

At the time, Van Velzen supported this revised church order. Above all, he wanted uniformity in the denomination, rather than the present situation in which each man was doing what was right in his own eyes in terms of church polity. In his introduction to the published *Acts of Synod*, President Van Velzen excoriated those who did not adhere to the decisions of the broader assemblies and the new church order, even going so far as to liken them to Korah, Dathan, and Abiram, whose rebellion so disturbed the church in the wilderness.[10] However, many were dissatisfied with this new church order, and some churches chose to flout this decision of synod.

While the debate over a new church order was being settled, synod also dealt with the matter of baptism. De Cock came to synod with a formal protest against the views of Scholte. The official minutes record that "the President [Van Velzen] admonishes De Cock to let those unfounded suspicions go and to work in fellowship for the building of Christ's body."[11]

Van Velzen later proposed that the newly adopted Church Order of Utrecht be prefaced by six doctrinal articles. Known later as "The Dogmatic Articles of Utrecht," these six theses adopted by synod addressed the matter of baptism and the related truth of the covenant and gave direction to the churches of the Afscheiding on this issue.[12]

1. All who make public confession of faith and walk in conformity therewith must with their children be acknowledged as members of the church of Christ.

---

10 Cf. *Handelingen en verslagen*, 79.
11 Quoted in Oostendorp, *H. P. Scholte*, 109.
12 E. Smilde, *Een eeuw van strijd over verbond en doop* [A century of conflict over covenant and baptism] (Kampen: J. H. Kok, 1946), 9.

2. Confession of faith consists in the agreement from the heart that is made public by the acknowledgment with the mouth of all the chief articles of the Christian religion. The walk of faith consists in forsaking the world and leading a life in agreement with God's commandments and in submission to the eternal king Jesus Christ.

3. Although there are hypocrites who are mixed in among the good, and it therefore is necessary and beneficial for each one to examine himself and to regard others; nevertheless, no one may be suspected of hypocrisy who makes this confession and leads a life of obedience.

4. The aforementioned confessors and their children must be continually acknowledged as members of the church, until they are cut off from the church because of their doctrine or walk.

5. As long as someone is not cut off from the congregation, he has the right to receive the signs and seals of the covenant of grace for himself and his seed; unless, however, the council of the church has placed him under censure for a time. The understanding, however, is that the censure has reference indeed to his person, but not to his seed.

6. Since the Lord Jesus Christ has been given all power in heaven and on earth, and because he has been by God specifically anointed as king over Zion, the mountain of his holiness, therefore no one, whether worldly government or any other man, may be permitted to exercise any power or authority in or upon the church.[13]

---

13 Quoted in Kamps, *1834*, 209. For the original text of these articles, cf. *Handelingen en verslagen*, 111–12; Smilde, *Een eeuw van strijd over verbond en doop*, 12–13.

There was much discussion over these articles, but the synod did finally make this significant pronouncement:

> The children of believers are included in the covenant of God and his congregation with their parents by virtue of the promises of God. Therefore, synod believes with Article 17 of Head 1 of the Canons of Dordt that godly parents must be admonished not to doubt the election and salvation of their children, whom God takes away in their infancy. Therefore, synod, with the baptism form, counts the children of believers to have to be regarded as members of the congregation of Christ, as heirs of the kingdom of God and of his covenant. Since, however, the word of God plainly teaches that not all are Israel who are of Israel, and the children of the promises are counted for the seed, therefore synod by no means regards all and every one head for head, whether children or adult confessors, as true objects of the grace of God or regenerated.[14]

The decisions made by the Synod of 1837 on these two important issues were, of course, divisive. De Cock was especially upset by what had taken place. He and a number of like-minded elders protested that the adoption of a new church order prefaced by the six dogmatic articles was completely unnecessary.

Those who protested were strongly influenced by the conventicles and the theology of the Dutch Further Reformation. The "custom in experientialist circles" was "to divide church members into converted and unconverted souls depending on all sorts of subjective characteristics."[15] For that reason, these men opposed

---

14 Quoted in David J. Engelsma, *Covenant and Election in the Reformed Tradition* (Jenison, MI: Reformed Free Publishing Association, 2011), 11.

15 Reenders, "Van Raalte," 282.

the synod's ruling that confessing members and their children were to be regarded as members of God's covenant as long as there was no evidence to the contrary.

But, a protest on the floor of synod was not the end of all disagreement. "After this Synod," Van Velzen recalled, "a few churches, ten in number, separated themselves and formed a distinct union, although there was no minister among them, but they soon appointed ministers out of their midst."[16] Toward the beginning of 1838, it was clear that many churches were not upholding the Church Order of Utrecht but instead were reverting back to the Church Order of Dordt. The group of ten churches, mostly from the northern provinces, finally separated from the denomination and formed the *Gereformeerde Kerken onder het Kruis*.[17]

Sadly, Hendrik de Cock was also persuaded to leave the denomination. But, he did not remain outside for very long. Albertus van Raalte made an emergency visit to De Cock and persuaded him to return shortly thereafter.

The loss of De Cock highlighted another objection that the *Kruisgezinden* (as the members were known) harbored. They were upset with the denomination's refusal to use oefenaars (lay preachers or exhorters). The first synod of the Afscheiding churches made a decision not to allow oefenaars in the churches.[18] Van Velzen especially was opposed to the use of these oefenaars. Although their inclusion would have swelled the ministerial ranks, it also would have undermined the lawful calling required for the office

---

16 Van Velzen, *Gedenkschrift der Christelijke Gereformeerde Kerk*, 113–14.
17 The ten churches were Zwolle, Deventer, Kampen, Hasselt, Zalk, Rouveen, Mastenbroek, Woerden, Linschoten, and Hattem. Cf. *Handelingen en verslagen*, 1158.
18 Cf. articles 34, 52, 56, 66, *Handelingen en verslagen*, 36, 45–48, 54.

of minister. Once De Cock returned to the denomination, the Kruisgezinden were left without any ordained ministers but only a number of oefenaars. In sheer desperation, one oefenaar (A. Schouwenberg) ordained two other men as lawful ministers (Wolter Wagter Smitt and Douwe Vander Werp), and then one of those men ordained the first man. This was certainly not the procedure outlined in their beloved Church Order of Dordt, but desperate times called for desperate measures.

According to one historian, this rupture took place because the Kruisgezinden failed to see the distinction between the Canons and the DKO. They wanted blind submission to everything that Dordt had decided: not just her doctrinal deliverances against the Remonstrants, but also her church political formulations. In this historian's judgment, such was evidence of an un-Reformed, radical conservatism.[19]

The first break had become reality. Besides the Hervormde Kerk, two distinct Reformed denominations now existed. But, this was not the end of the divisions. Another painful separation would soon take place, with Van Velzen playing a leading role.

---

19 Te Velde, *Anthony Brummelkamp*, 101.

Chapter 9

———⟫❁⟪———

THE AMSTERDAM TWIST

*T*he vacant congregation in the city of Amsterdam was the site of the second fierce conflict that convulsed the churches of the Afscheiding.

Amsterdam, the bustling capital of the Netherlands and the birthplace of Van Velzen, did not have an Afscheiding church until a year after the reformation began. In October 1835, Hendrik Scholte organized the first Secession church of Amsterdam. Since he was responsible for the labors in North Holland, the province in which the capital was found, it fell to Scholte to take charge of the group there, although technically they were without a pastor of their own.

Still, the church grew rapidly, and soon three hundred souls were counted on the church roll. Part of the reason for her quick growth was the fact that the church was not persecuted as heavily as her sister congregations in other parts of the country were. The city officials in Amsterdam interpreted the Napoleonic Code differently than their colleagues in other cities and allowed the saints to gather in worship without fear of interruption.

Amsterdam church building interior

Besides her relatively large size, the church in Amsterdam was characterized by a lack of internal unity. Since Amsterdam was a bustling metropolis and a magnet for immigrants, the church was not homogeneous but consisted of a number of different groups. This undoubtedly played a role in the later divisions that rocked the congregation.

Some of these divisions were the remnants of two earlier conventicles, one led by Coenrad Deteleff and the other by Harm Hendrik Middel, both of whom later became elders in the church. Van Velzen's mother was a member of the congregation and was active in the conventicle of Middel. Members of her conventicle were strong supporters of her son. And increasingly, they were becoming dissatisfied with Scholte, with Middel even charging Scholte with being a Remonstrant after a sermon he preached.

Van Velzen likely heard reports of the goings-on in Amsterdam from his mother, and he was steadily becoming unhappy with Scholte's role there. These divisions in Amsterdam were representative of a broader tension that was growing between these two leaders of the Afscheiding. A main cause of their conflict was Scholte's attitude of independentism. As one writer put it, Van Velzen "was beginning to discover that Scholte was the fly in the ointment of synodical peace."[1]

One way in which Scholte revealed his independent spirit at this time was in the matter of government recognition.[2] The government refused to recognize the denomination as legitimate churches. This meant that their worship services were unlawful, and anyone found participating was subject to punishment. Many of the seceders faced fines and imprisonment.

They could have easily brought an end to this situation. The king had decreed that if the seceders would relinquish any claim to the name and property of the Dutch Reformed Church, he would recognize them and the persecution would come to an abrupt end. However, the seceders deemed this unacceptable. The reason they had seceded in the first place was not to start a new denomination but to preserve the Reformed church. So, they refused to cave in to the king and surrender the name *Reformed*.

But then, out of the blue and without a word of warning to any of the others, Scholte and the church in Utrecht applied for government recognition in the fall of 1838. They renounced the name *Reformed* and applied for recognition as a "Christian Seceded Church." This request was officially approved by the Ministry of Religion in February 1839. Now Scholte and his church were recognized and free of opposition, while Van Velzen and the others continued to bear the brunt of the persecution.

---

1 Oostendorp, *H. P. Scholte*, 116.
2 For this section on government recognition, cf. Reenders, "Van Raalte," 285–88.

This was just one instance of Scholte's independent spirit and Van Velzen's growing disillusionment with his colleague. The issues between the two had been smoldering for a while and now would finally erupt in Amsterdam.

The first phase of their conflict—known as the "first Amsterdam dispute (*eerste Amsterdamsche twist*)"—stemmed from the decisions of Synod 1837 regarding the church order. The synod had adopted a new church order—the Church Order of Utrecht—and Van Velzen was its primary proponent. Behind this position was Van Velzen's stubborn insistence upon the real, binding authority of the broader assemblies (the classis, provincial synod, and general synod). He was adamant that since synod had approved this church order, the churches must all accept and use it. Failure to do so would mean the disintegration of denominational unity.

Scholte disagreed. He rejected the authority of the synod. He thought that synod could give advice, but such advice had no teeth. Each congregation could decide for itself whether to take the advice or leave it. He continued to drift further and further in the direction of independentism.

These issues came to roost in Amsterdam in the early part of 1838, when Van Velzen first became involved with the congregation there. At that time, he was called upon to install new elders in the congregation. But, these elders unashamedly made known that they would not accept the new church order approved by synod, in so doing revealing the same independent spirit as their founder, Scholte. Van Velzen, dogged defender of denominational unity that he was, responded by refusing to install these men into office. This action immediately put him at odds with a sizable chunk of the congregation. One man criticized, "Van

Velzen has something absolute in his personality. The one who stands in his way must be made innocuous."[3]

Yet, a majority of that vacant congregation respected Van Velzen and stood with him. This was plain from the fact that they extended a call to him later in the year. On October 5, 1838, the church sent a call letter to Scholte. He would have been inclined to accept the call, since he viewed Amsterdam as one of his own congregations. However, Scholte declined it instead. He did so because he had received only 27 out of 108 votes at the congregational meeting, and since this did not constitute a majority, he felt that the call was not legitimate. Amsterdam held another congregational meeting on November 28, at which time Scholte received 27 votes out of a total of 68 while Van Velzen received 32 votes. Since there was still not a clear majority, the men voted again, and on the second ballot Scholte received 33 votes and Van Velzen received 35. A call (with a proposed salary of 1,200 guilders) was extended, therefore, to Van Velzen rather than Scholte. Scholte was likely confused and a little upset by the outcome.

A tremendous struggle took place in Van Velzen's heart and mind over whether to accept this call. He was inclined not to accept because of the severe shortage of pastors in Friesland. However, the situation changed while Van Velzen was still considering Amsterdam's call. At the end of 1838, R. W. Duin was called to be the second minister in Friesland, and on January 22, 1839, he was installed into office by Van Velzen.[4] With his concerns

---

3 Harm Bouwman, quoted in Heideman, *Hendrik P. Scholte*, 132.
4 Wormser, *Karakter en genade*, 39; Smits, *De Afscheiding van 1834*, 3:140. Swierenga says that Duin "shared Scholte's views." He was "an Ost Frisian Seceder from the German Reformed Church who from 1839 to 1841 co-pastored with van Velzen the Seceder churches in Friesland, Groningen,

about Friesland (temporarily) alleviated, Van Velzen sent a letter on January 28 to the church in Amsterdam, informing them that he had accepted their call.

The situation became messy after Van Velzen announced his acceptance of Amsterdam's call. Instead of leaving Friesland and taking up residence in Amsterdam, Van Velzen and his family remained in Friesland. Van Velzen traveled to Amsterdam alone and met with the consistory on February 15. He informed them that he was unable to move, but then he preached for them two days later and announced to the congregation that he had in fact accepted their call. The members of the church in Amsterdam were understandably confused.

Van Velzen explained to the consistory and congregation that he had not fully understood their intentions when they called him. He did not realize that they wanted to have him all to themselves. He understood the call to mean rather that he would serve the church in Amsterdam while continuing to perform his labors among the Frisian congregations.[5] If he had

---

and Drenthe. Duin, with more lax German roots, soon became a big problem. He challenged the doctrines of election and reprobation as defined in the Canons, approved hymn singing, and refused to discipline parishioners who conducted necessary business on Sunday. De Cock and van Velzen came to view Duin as a traitor to the Secession and after two years of bitter controversy at church assemblies, managed to expel him. [Herbert] Brinks argues that the 'Duin case' stiffened the spine of the northern wing of the Afscheiding for years and shaped the thinking of immigrants in this tradition, such as the Drenthers and Graafschapers in Michigan in the 1850s. Dort's church rules became the bulwark for preserving the 'essentiality of the 1834 secession.'" Cf. Swierenga, *Family Quarrels*, 28n29. Swierenga refers to Herbert J. Brinks, "Another Look at 1857: The Birth of the CRC," *Origins* 4, no. 1 (1986): 27–31.

5 Even when he was installed as Amsterdam's pastor, Van Velzen continued to identify himself as "pastor and teacher of the Christian Secession Church in Friesland and Amsterdam." Cf. Tjoelker, *Ds. S. van Velzen*, 68.

known their intentions, he never would have taken their call. He still felt bound to Friesland because of the scarcity of ministers, but when there were more ministers, he would readily be bound to one place.

In light of Van Velzen's difficulties, the consistory called a congregational meeting to decide how to proceed. At that meeting 68 members voted to approve Van Velzen's acceptance of their call, while 11 members, including one elder, protested. Van Velzen was still called.

Now, Van Velzen faced objections from the other side. Some of the saints in Friesland were unwilling to let their beloved pastor leave. Three men brought protests to the Provincial Synod of Friesland against Van Velzen's departure. Despite their love for Van Velzen, the provincial synod declared "that Rev. van Velzen is completely free to serve the congregation of Amsterdam as her own pastor and teacher...Rev. van Velzen promised, nevertheless, to continue as much as possible to serve the province of Friesland as pastor and teacher."[6]

After many months of controversy, Van Velzen was finally able to move his family to Amsterdam. His work as Amsterdam's pastor officially began on June 16, when he was installed by Hendrik de Cock. Van Velzen was indeed coming home. Not only was he returning to the city of his birth and childhood, but, as was noted earlier, he was returning to the very house in which he was raised. His family home had become the church building and parsonage of Amsterdam's congregation.

---

6   Smits, *De Afscheiding van 1834*, 3:141, 5:123. The three men who protested Van Velzen's departure were W. D. Hellema (from Wirdum), J. Meijering (from Leeuwarden), and Pier Ottes de Jong (from Wolvega).

Willem Hendrik Gispen

Willem Hendrik Gispen (1833–1909), a son of the congregation and later a prominent minister in the churches,[7] reminisced on Van Velzen's ministry in Amsterdam after his death:

We still see Van Velzen as he rises from the ground and through a hole—that after coming through it was closed with a hatch, and on which a few ladies, most of them wives of the consistory members, sat down—appeared in the congregation of the faithful, clothed in the dignified ministerial garb of the first half of this century. We still hear the elongated votum and the lingering tone in which the Psalm verse was recited. At that time we had no understanding of the neatness in the style and the beautiful construction of the sentences, nor of the mechanics of the sermon, to which Van Velzen always took great care. But we had deep reverence in the heart for the Reverend, who was presented to us by our parents and others as a servant of Christ, who had fought and suffered much for the sake of the truth and who appeared before our eyes with the crown of glory of the martyr. We felt honored when he came on house visitation with an elder, and especially our hearts trembled when he, with his hat in hand, entered

---

7   Gispen entered the ministry in the Kruisgezinden via article 8, which allows a man with singular gifts to enter the ministry without formal training. He served the Kruisgezinden in De Lier and Vlissingen and then led the Vlissingen congregation back into the Secession churches in 1860. He then served congregations in Giessendam, Kampen (1864–73), and Amsterdam.

the catechism room and we would sit close to him and answer the questions he asked us in response to an article from the [Belgic] Confession of Faith. Because Van Velzen did not use catechism books in his teaching, but only the confessions of the church, nor did he drill the catechumens in all kinds of theological subjects, but simply prepared us for the Lord's Supper."[8]

◆ ◆ ◆

The first months of his pastorate in Amsterdam were not easy. After the loss of his first wife in the early days of the Afscheiding, Van Velzen somehow found time in the busyness of his work to court a woman and marry again. On June 2, 1838, barely a year since his first wife died, he was joined in marriage to Johanna Alijda Lucia van Voss, who also came from a notable family. She was the sister-in-law of Carel de Moen, Van Velzen's brother-in-law by his first marriage.[9] It was likely through this connection that the two of them met. Shortly before the marriage, Van Velzen wrote to Scholte to inform him of the impending union: "I wrote this to inform you that I am betrothed to J. A. L. van Voss, the sister-in-law of my brother-in-law De Moen of Hattem. I believe in doing this matter according to the Lord's will, and I hope that our beginning will be in his fear and favor."[10] Sadly, Simon and Johanna did not have long together. On October 17, 1839, just a few months after coming to Amsterdam, Johanna gave birth to a stillborn child. This was not an uncommon occurrence at that time, but it was a heartbreaking loss nonetheless. Simon's

---

8   Quoted in Van Gelderen, *Simon van Velzen*, 35–36.
9   Bruins, *Albertus and Christina*, 206. Van Velzen's second wife was the younger sister of Carel de Moen's wife, Agatha Sophia van Voss.
10 Quoted in Smits, *De Afscheiding van 1834*, 3:133.

grief was compounded by the fact that Johanna died that same day due to complications from the pregnancy. Once again, Van Velzen had to bury loved ones. Once again, he and his young son, Simon, were left alone.

Added to this personal grief was the continuation of the conflict with Scholte. Another, more bitter chapter in the controversy had begun, a chapter that became known as the "second Amsterdam dispute (*tweede Amsterdamsche twist*)."

On December 6, Van Velzen and the Amsterdam consistory wrote a letter to Scholte and the consistory of the church in Utrecht. In this letter, they objected to Scholte's actions in examining two young men and ordaining them into the ministry without ever consulting the broader assemblies. Any student who wanted to enter the ministry had to be examined first by a synodical committee, a committee of which Van Velzen was a member.[11]

Scholte and his consistory fired back immediately. In a letter dated December 18, the Utrecht consistory did not simply take a defensive stance, but they went on the offensive against Van Velzen. They charged him with preaching dry doctrines rather than the gospel. The letter they drafted said, "[Van Velzen] preaches a conglomeration of theoretical truths without the living Christ, without a regenerating Spirit, and without the living and active faith."[12] They accused Van Velzen of being "duplicitous, quarrelsome, and imperious."[13]

Scholte had the nerve to deliver the letter himself. He appeared before the Amsterdam consistory on December 21 and

---

11 Smits, *De Afscheiding van 1834*, 5:122. The two young men whom Scholte examined and ordained were H. G. Klijn and C. van der Meulen.
12 Quoted in Oostendorp, *H. P. Scholte*, 122.
13 Quoted in Heideman, *Hendrik P. Scholte*, 132.

read aloud the objections against Van Velzen. But, Van Velzen was not even there to hear the charges leveled by his colleague; he was in Friesland carrying out work that the churches there had requested of him. When asked where he had heard such things about Van Velzen, Scholte replied that he was the source. Shortly before, he had come to Amsterdam to sit in the pew to hear Van Velzen preach and had brought back the charges to the Utrecht consistory.

Things continued to spiral out of control in the new year. Van Velzen remained in Friesland through the holidays and therefore was not present when the consistory gathered on January 3, 1840, to deal again with Scholte's objections. Since Van Velzen was not there to chair the meeting, this duty fell to Elder D. A. Budde. But another elder (W. de Haas) objected to his leading the meeting, so Elder J. C. Couprie was asked to preside.[14] During the course of the meeting, Elder Budde and another elder (J. A. Wormser) as well as two deacons (D. Lijsen and H. Höveker) expressed the thought that Scholte's objections had some merit and were worth further investigation. One of these elders later wrote, in language reminiscent of Scholte's letter, that Van Velzen "does not rightly divide the Word, hides the intention of the Word, and instead of calling and attracting sinners to Christ, which is the calling of a minister of the Gospel, he buries them under a pile of doctrines which are in themselves orthodox and thus lets them go. By this the God-opposing practice is fed, to blame the lack of actual faith and the exercise of faith to a lack of grace, instead of placing

---

14 Wormser, *Karakter en genade*, 46–47. Wormser gives the date of the meeting as January 8. Others have confirmed that the date was January 3. Cf. Te Velde, *Anthony Brummelkamp*, 122; Smits, *De Afscheiding van 1834*, 5:123.

the guilt upon man."[15] Another made the wild claim that Van Velzen was unconverted.[16] The rest of the consistory, however, decided that Scholte and his consistory had slandered Van Velzen and judged that the objections did not have merit. Because the dissenting elders and deacons refused to abide by this decision, they were suspended by the rest of the consistory.

These four officebearers refused to acknowledge their suspension. In turn, they suspended Van Velzen and the officebearers faithful to him and referred to themselves as the true Amsterdam consistory. They began holding separate worship services with their supporters and even extended a call to Scholte to be their minister. A few weeks later, Scholte preached for this group and administered the sacrament of the Lord's supper to them. One of them (J. A. Wormser) began airing the dirty laundry between the congregations on the pages of the denominational magazine *De Reformatie*. The fissure between the two parties in Amsterdam and between the two fathers of the Afscheiding was deepening.

Van Velzen's and Scholte's colleagues were not oblivious to the seriousness of the situation. Their old friend Brummelkamp stepped in to try to resolve the affair, calling an unofficial meeting of ministers and elders in Amsterdam from March 6–7, 1840. At the meeting Scholte was unable satisfactorily to prove his assertion that Van Velzen's preaching was void of the gospel. So, Brummelkamp and the others demanded three things of Scholte:

1. Recognition of unlawful interference in the acceptance of Amsterdam's call by Rev. van Velzen;
2. Retraction of the objections against Rev. van Velzen's preaching; and

---

15 Quoted in Oostendorp, *H. P. Scholte*, 123.
16 Oostendorp, *H. P. Scholte*, 124.

3. Recognition of unlawful action in causing a schism in the congregation of Amsterdam.[17]

Scholte refused to do as they asked. Therefore, the whole matter came to the meeting of synod later that year.

The delegates met in Amsterdam from November 17 to December 3, with Brummelkamp serving as president. Worth noting is the fact that synod scrapped the previous church order it had adopted and instead decided to revert to using the Church Order of Dordt. Synod said:

> We also declare that we recognize the Dort Church Order with abolition of all that was ever produced before regarding Church Orders, judging and hoping that such may be to the edification of the congregations of the Lord. For a considerable time this has led to discord in the congregations, and outside of them it was already said that the Seceders, as many others, busied themselves with making innovations. And, however much we may be convinced in our hearts that we aimed at the edification of the congregations, we could not escape this accusation…Let no one think, however, that with this Church Order, we would impose a yoke upon the churches. No; we want to show hereby that it is our only aim to associate ourselves as closely as possible with the government, discipline, and ministry as our forefathers put it.[18]

The main thing before the synod, however, was the issue of Scholte. Scholte refused to appear at synod, despite his involvement in the whole affair. Because of his refusal, synod tasked

---

17 *Handelingen en verslagen*, 188. Cf. Oostendorp, *H. P. Scholte*, 124.
18 Quoted in Pronk, *A Goodly Heritage*, 186–87.

Hendrik de Cock with hunting him down and speaking with him. De Cock did so, calling Scholte to repent of his wrongdoing in the matter with Van Velzen as well as to submit himself to the Church Order of Dordt. Scholte refused, and synod took the sad step of deposing him from office.[19]

Although he was deposed, Scholte still found many supporters within the denomination. Most congregations recognized his deposition, but some churches disregarded this decision and still invited Scholte to fill their pulpits. Even though Scholte was permitted to appear at the next meeting of synod in 1843, a second, definite break had taken place in the churches of the Afscheiding.

Scholte's deposition marked the decline of his influence in the Afscheiding churches. Because of his ecclesiastical position and other economic factors, Scholte and a group of supporters set sail for America on April 8, 1847. They eventually settled on the open fields of Iowa and established the town of Pella. Scholte never lost his independent spirit, and as a result, he caused many headaches for the settlers in Pella.

Although the Amsterdam affair was a painful, messy ordeal for Van Velzen and the denomination, it proved in the providence of God to be beneficial for the churches. Scholte had revealed a radical and independent mindset that did not promote peace and unity in the truth. He denied the authority of broader assemblies. And already in 1838, Scholte was in correspondence with John Nelson Darby, the founder of dispensational premillennialism, which teaching Scholte himself would later espouse. Scholte's removal from the churches served

---

19 Oostendorp, *H. P. Scholte*, 125–27. This is not the place to debate the legality (or illegality) of a broader ecclesiastical assembly deposing a minister.

to preserve and unite them. Both Van Velzen and Scholte can be faulted for certain of their actions in this conflict; nevertheless, God overruled these faults and used this incident to strengthen the churches of the Secession. This is often the way that God is pleased to work in his church. He strengthens and purifies her in the crucible of controversy.

Chapter 10

THE ROBBERS
SYNOD

*A*mid all the troubles and sorrows of his labors in the churches, Van Velzen once again knew joy in his personal life. On September 1, 1841, he married for the third time. His wife was named Zwaantje Stratingh, who hailed from Delfzijl, Groningen, a fishing village hard against the North Sea. Her father was a sea captain. Their marriage lasted longer than Van Velzen's previous two combined. God blessed their marriage with eight children, although their joy was tempered by the loss of two who died while young. The six remaining children were Johanna Neeltje, Margaretha, Jacobus (who became an engineer), Joannes (who became a soldier), Geertruida Maria, and Jurrien Hendrik. Interestingly, their three daughters all later married ministers.

A little over a year after this marriage, Van Velzen experienced the death of another person with whom he was close: Hendrik de Cock. Throughout the early years of the Afscheiding, Hendrik de Cock was the *primus inter pares*, the unquestioned leader among the many capable men in the churches. He was the first to secede from the mother church and was influential in leading others out of her bosom as well. In subsequent years, his colleagues in the ministry frequently looked to him for guidance. It was therefore

a sad day in the churches of the Afscheiding when De Cock died. On Sunday, November 14, 1842, at eight o'clock in the morning, De Cock passed from the earthly Sabbath into the eternal Sabbath.

Van Velzen had been close to De Cock, so De Cock's widow, the pious Frouwe Venema, sent him a letter informing him of her husband's death. Shortly thereafter, Van Velzen preached a memorial sermon to his congregation in Amsterdam from Revelation 14:13, taking as his theme "De

Frouwe de Cock

Zalige Dooden" ("The Blessedness of the Dead"). The lengthy quotation that follows is from that sermon, which quotation is included not only for what it says about De Cock but also about the preaching ability of Van Velzen:

> When we, consequently, consider this incomparable privilege of the blessed, then we have reason to rejoice regarding them, while faced with their death. We have therefore also reason concerning our beloved brother, the now-deceased shepherd and pastor De Cock, to call him blessed, who has been released from the battle, who had found his deliverance from guilt and punishment in the imputed righteousness of Christ, and who to the end of his life, even as his sorrowing wife wrote to me, was privileged to look to Christ, who now has cleansed his servant from the stain of sin. Remember them, according to the admonition of the apostle, which have the rule over you,

who have spoken unto you the word of God: whose faith follow, considering the end of their walk. For him, Rev. H. de Cock, this change is inexpressibly blessed; but we suffer a great loss.

Not only were we privileged a few times to hear him preach the gospel of grace from this pulpit, but you will also remember how he combined genuine simplicity with profound earnestness in his preaching and how he without ostentation but with strong words preached this necessary element of faith and then another necessary aspect. He not only labored in that part of the country where the Lord had specifically placed him and where he was active in many congregations, but he was used as the leader for the entire Secession church in our country.

He was the first pastor who publicly and without any duplicity exposed, reproved, rejected, and resisted the evil that had acquired dominance in the church. He was the first who was faithful, who joined the battle not only in words but also in deeds for the truth and for the rights of truly Reformed believers, and who remained faithful and demonstrated that he had abandoned all self interests for this cause. He was the first who, after exhausting every avenue for the restoration of the true Reformed church, at last rejected that rule of the church that had trampled under foot the rights of Reformed believers. But he did so only after witnessing the failure of every attempt at restoration because of the obstinacy of the enemies of the truth and the pure worship of God. He was the first to forsake that fellowship that we could no longer acknowledge as the true Reformed church, as the church of Christ.

The zeal that began with him inspired many. God used him as the most prominent pillar. Through his leadership this work quickly prospered. Courageously he fought the battle against unbelief and the world to the very end. He worked tirelessly for the building up of Zion; he showed himself prepared to suffer for it. He was defamed, summoned before the judgment seats, cast into prison, robbed of his possessions, and his life was threatened, yet he remained steadfast and always pleasant. Departure from pure doctrine and the proven paths of our fathers he did not view indifferently; on the contrary, he was always ready to defend the truth and our fathers' walk of faith. But when division and arguments arose among brothers, he was always busy attempting to work reconciliation.

We must say of him: By faith…choosing rather to suffer affliction with the people of God, than to enjoy the pleasures of sin for a season; esteeming the reproach of Christ as greater riches than the treasures of the world. He fought the good fight and kept the faith. Of him we have to say that he labored more than all the others. If such a servant of God is taken to heaven, and indeed at the specific moment when the church is besieged in so many different ways, then we have reason, following the example of King Joash, to cry out at his departure: "My father, My father, the chariot of Israel, and the horsemen thereof!" However, God's doing is majesty; he dwells in his holy temple. It is fitting therefore that we be silent before him. If we consider, beloved, that our life is but a handbreadth; before we expected it, we have reached the boundary marker between life and death; blessed are the

dead then who die in the Lord, but those who have slandered him will be lightly esteemed.[1]

With the death of De Cock, the mantle of the leadership of
the churches, especially those in the northern provinces, fell to
Van Velzen. It was in this capacity that he became involved in
another painful controversy, one that wracked the churches of the
Afscheiding for more than a decade.

◆ ◆ ◆

Despite the positive effects it had, the Synod of 1840 was not able
to heal all the divisions in the churches. In fact, it can be argued
that just as many problems existed after the synod as before. Two
issues in particular remained unresolved.

First, the question of Scholte's status still lingered in the
minds of some. Some refused to acknowledge his deposition and
encouraged him to continue laboring in the churches.

Second, the matter of the church order was still a major bone
of contention. Synod 1840 had appeased many by returning to
the Church Order of Dordt, but at the same time this decision
upset others, particularly Brummelkamp and Van Raalte. They
felt that the decision to return to the Church Order of Dordt
was done out of a slavish sense of traditionalism. Following these
leaders, many churches simply refused to use this Church Order.
When these refusals became known in the denomination, the situation created a further firestorm over the proper interpretation
of article 31 of the Church Order when it says that "whatever
may be agreed upon by a majority vote shall be considered settled

---

1 Van Velzen, *De zalige dooden, predicatie bij gelegenheid vna het afsterven van
den weleerwaarden heer H. de Cock* [The blessedness of the dead, a sermon
at the occasion of the decease of the highly esteemed pastor H. de Cock] ('s

and binding, unless it be proved to conflict with the Word of God or with the articles of the Church Order." Men like Van Velzen interpreted this to mean that the decisions of the broader assemblies—such as the decision of Synod 1840 to use the Church Order of Dordt—are binding in the churches. Others said that there was freedom to disregard a decision if they felt it was contrary to the word of God or did not serve the edification of their congregation. This would become the central issue that divided the churches.

These issues festered under the surface of the churches for the next three years. At one point, Brummelkamp wrote to Van Raalte that he did not feel bound to the Church Order of Dordt and that he planned to have more interaction with Scholte. At a provincial synod that Brummelkamp chaired and at which his brother-in-law, Carel de Moen, was examined for the ministry, Brummelkamp made a point of refusing to ask De Moen to sign the DKO. Brummelkamp's wife also confided to her sister, Van Raalte's wife, "With respect to the Church Order of Dort, we live in freedom and joy. Oh, fortunately, to us it is only a matter of incidentals."[2]

It was only a matter of time before these issues burst forth and created another division in the denomination, which took place at the Synod of 1843.

In the summer of 1843, Anthony Brummelkamp recognized the need for another national synod and called the churches to deal with these issues. The synod convened on July 26 in Amsterdam with forty-three men present, including Scholte and several

Gravenhage: J. van Golverdinge, 1842), 25–28. I have used the translation of Kamps, *1834*, 197–99.

2   Quoted in Reenders, "Van Raalte," 290n50. Brummelkamp's letter to Van Raalte was dated March 17, 1842. The letter of Brummelkamp's wife to her sister was dated December 20, 1842.

of his supporters. Already at the opening session, there was evidence of dissension among the ranks. The delegates could not agree on the basis for the gathering.

Three basic groups were present. The first group consisted of the delegates from North Holland, Groningen, Drenthe, Friesland, and South Holland, and they called for adherence to the Church Order of Dordt. Van Velzen belonged to this group. The second group, made of delegates from Zeeland as well as the supporters of Scholte in Utrecht and South Holland, did not want to be bound by the Church Order of Dordt. The third group, made of men from the southern provinces of Gelderland, Overijssel, and North Brabant, attempted to pacify the two other groups and bring everyone together. Brummelkamp and Van Raalte belonged to this latter group.

For two whole days, the delegates went back and forth over this issue. At the same time the assembly deliberated whether to recognize Scholte's presence since he had been deposed at the previous synod. Van Raalte especially pushed for the synod to welcome him. In the end, no resolution was achieved. In frustration, Scholte and his followers left, as did Brummelkamp, Van Raalte, and the delegates from Overijssel, Gelderland, and North Brabant. In all, twenty-two delegates walked out, leaving only twenty-one men behind. These remaining delegates chose Van Velzen as president and carried out the rest of the business of the synod. This is considered by many to be the low point in the history of the Afscheiding churches, and the Synod of 1843 has since been dubbed the "Robbers Synod," an allusion to the supposedly illegal character of the continued meeting.[3]

From that point on, two different parties existed among the

---

3   Te Velde, *Anthony Brummelkamp*, 138–39; Wormser, *Karakter en genade*, 60–64. The Dutch is "Roovers-Synode."

churches of the Afscheiding. One party, the party that stood for many years outside the main line of the Afscheiding churches, was known as the *Gelderse richting* (Gelderland party). This party consisted of thirteen churches in the province of Gelderland, seven churches in Overijssel, and a few churches in Zeeland. This group was led by the three brothers-in-law: Brummelkamp, Van Raalte, and Carel de Moen.

Hendrik Joffers

Tamme Foppes de Haan

Those recognized as standing in the line of De Cock and the Afscheiding were predominantly found in the northern provinces and became known as the *Drentse richting* (Drenthe party). The most outspoken (and at times extreme) leaders of this group were Hendrik Joffers (1807–74), Frederik Alberts Kok (1803–60), and Tamme Foppes de Haan (1791–1868). In certain respects these men were heavily influenced by the Dutch Further Reformation. Van Velzen's name was often associated with this group, and in many ways he was one with them. Nevertheless, it is generally recognized that he did not belong wholly to it and did not condone their more extreme sentiments.[4]

Robert Swierenga characterizes the two parties this way. He says that Van Velzen and the northern party "defended the doctrine,

---

4   Veenhof, *Prediking en uitverkiezing*, 13–16. Although Veenhof expresses sharp disagreement with Van Velzen and with the Drentse richting, he does acknowledge that Van Velzen was too Reformed and had too broad a view of the church and her calling in the world to belong wholly to the Drentse (cf. p. 15).

liturgy, and polity of Dort as biblically grounded; they were strongly traditional Calvinists who stressed the need for Christian schools and catechetical instruction of the youth, given the 'Godless influence' in the public schools." In contrast, the southern wing, heavily influenced by Brummelkamp, was "more broadminded, inclusive, and even-tempered; it stressed experiential piety and evangelism to the point that some charged them with Arminian leanings." Swierenga concludes, "The northern faction had steel in their bones, while the southern party had rubber."[5]

One of the underlying issues dividing these two parties that later came to light had to do with the preaching. In particular, the two sides were divided over the so-called "well-meant offer of the gospel."[6] The introduction of this well-meant offer into the churches of the Afscheiding was due primarily to Anthony Brummelkamp. Already in September 1841, some of Brummelkamp's parishioners objected to his preaching of the well-meant offer. Others in the churches agreed that "the offer of grace was too broad in his preaching. Sometimes it was as if a man could just accept the grace because God promised it. The word Remonstrantism was used."[7] Van Velzen and the others of the Drentse richting strongly opposed this idea. This became the impetus for some to label the two groups the "Van Velzian" or "strict-Reformed" party and the "Brummelkampian" or "Semi-Arminian" party.[8]

Surprisingly, another issue that divided the two parties had to do with the distinctive clothing worn by a minister. Reenders explains, "The faction of the old pious people insisted that

5   Swierenga and Bruins, *Family Quarrels*, 33–34.
6   Algra, *Het wonder van de 19e eeuw*, 151; Herman Hanko, "The *Afscheiding* and the Well-Meant Gospel Offer," in *Always Reforming*, 74–78.
7   Algra, *Het wonder van de 19e eeuw*, 154.
8   Wormser, *Karakter en genade*, 90.

ministers should wear the clerical garb, that is, knickerbockers, a black cloak with bands, and a cocked hat. They regarded this clerical garb as a sign of orthodoxy and of the office's loftiness. The cocked hat was even seen by some as a symbol of the Trinity."[9] It had long been expected of ministers that they wear this special clothing not only when they were leading worship services but also whenever they appeared in public. This clerical costume had been the clothing worn by all respectable citizens in the previous century, but had long gone out of style by the time of the Secession. In general, the men of the Drentse richting were in favor of maintaining the ministerial garb, while the men of the Gelderse richting were in favor of casting it off.

Recognizing the strong opinions on this matter, the Synod of 1840 advised (but did not require) ministers to wear the distinctive clothing in order not to give offense. This decision did not remedy the situation. Many thought the synod should have come down more firmly in favor of ministerial garb, while others thought synod went too far. A few years later, the Provincial Synod of Gelderland approached the neighboring province of Overijssel with a request to join them in petitioning the national synod to discard the ministerial garb. Debate on the floor of the meeting was vehement, with equal supporters on both sides. No decision was made at that meeting, and the synod which met that year did not address the issue either. However, the Synod of Groningen in 1846 made a decision requiring ministers to wear the special garb in congregations where discarding it would cause offense.

Synod's decision was not warmly received by all, particularly by ministers and congregations in the provinces of Gelderland and Overijssel. So divisive was the issue that from 1847 on, an

---

9   Reenders, "Van Raalte," 295.

actual split existed between the congregations in those provinces. Those of the Drentse richting held their own separate provincial synods in the city of Zwolle, and those of the Gelderse richting did the same in the city of Arnhem.

This split in the churches between Drentse and Gelderse soon became acrimonious. The weekly newspaper in the churches was *De Bazuin* (*The Trumpet*), which at the time was edited by Brummelkamp, Van Raalte, and De Moen. A second magazine, *De Stem* (*The Voice*), appeared during this time with Joffers as editor.[10] In his magazine, Joffers spoke strongly against the Gelderse. Once, referring to them as "nephews," he called the churches in strong poetry to, "Watch and drive the nephews out, before you become the heretic's bride."[11] Following his lead, the Drentse said that the Gelderse were not Reformed in doctrine or church polity and closed their pulpits and Lord's supper tables to them.

From the other side, Van Velzen was largely shunned by his former friends and fellow leaders of the Afscheiding. Brummelkamp referred to him as the fifth wheel on the wagon and refused to have anything to do with him.[12] The same was true of Van Raalte, who was drawn to the city of Arnhem in 1844 by Brummelkamp in order to help in the work of training ministerial students there. Interestingly, these two also maintained a close

---

10 Veenhof, *Prediking en uitverkiezing*, 11, 143–44. Later, Van Velzen would become editor of *De Bazuin* along with his fellow professors at Kampen, and he would bemoan the presence of multiple papers in the denomination, believing that there ought to be only one. Cf. Veenhof, *Prediking en uitverkiezing*, 146–47.

11 Quoted in Veenhof, *Prediking en uitverkiezing*, 22.

12 Te Velde, *Anthony Brummelkamp*, 141. It is interesting to consider whether the loss of Van Velzen's first wife at a young age and his subsequent remarriages weakened his relationship to Brummelkamp, Van Raalte, and De Moen, while that continuing family bond strengthened the relationship between the other three.

relationship with Scholte. Brummelkamp was even interested in having Scholte join him at his school in Arnhem and wrote to Van Raalte, "Is it not foolish to let Scholte with all his talents be discarded and ignored because he is still in trouble, while at the same time we feel we are in trouble up to our ears?"[13] Brummelkamp allowed Scholte to preach for him in Arnhem in 1844, and in 1845 he presided at the wedding ceremony of Scholte and his second wife, Mariah Krantz.[14]

The breach between Van Velzen and Van Raalte widened when the latter left for America. Van Raalte sailed from Rotterdam on October 2, 1846, leading a group of immigrants who would eventually establish the colony of Holland, Michigan. Although other factors were involved in Van Raalte's immigration (not least of which was that the church in Arnhem was unable to support him financially), one that is often overlooked is the fact that he stood outside the fellowship of the Afscheiding churches and was grieved by this division. Several years later, Van Raalte wrote, "The dissensions among the believers in the Netherlands caused me constantly a deep sorrow. They were harder for me to bear than the persecution; they deprived me of all enjoyment of life and made me

Hendrik Scholte

---

13 Quoted in Robert P. Swierenga, "Van Raalte and Scholte: A Soured Relationship and Personal Rivalry," *Origins* 17, no. 1 (1999): 24.

14 Te Velde, *Anthony Brummelkamp*, 141. For a brief introduction to the spirited Mariah, cf. Muriel Byers Kooi, "Solving a Problem Like Mareah," *Origins* 15, no. 1 (1997): 19–21.

afraid of life."[15] He wanted to free the immigrants not only from financial poverty and government persecution, but also from "the isolated state and ignorant dissension and narrow sectarian spirit by which the otherwise splendid people of the Seceders corrupt themselves" and "have become a prey to the follies of earlier and later leaders."[16]

The events that took place in the Secession churches during these decades (from about 1840 to 1890) are largely unknown to most people today.[17] This may be due to the fact that during this time, Van Raalte and Scholte immigrated to America, and many take interest in what happened to them there rather than events back in the Netherlands. The reason may also be that this history is filled with bitter infighting, which some conclude was petty and involved unnecessary hairsplitting.[18]

As painful as this history was, it is important to know in order to fully understand what was happening in the churches at that time. And, it is important to know because these debates and divisions would linger in Dutch Reformed circles on both sides of the Atlantic well into the twentieth century.

This history is also significant because it highlights an important truth about the church: she is reformed and preserved by the grace of God. If left to men, the church would tear herself apart and be utterly destroyed. One Secession minister said of this time, "If the Secession had been a work of men, there would surely have been nothing but fragments and splinters of the outgoing church left. But God is faithful; He holds His work in life, though He allowed Satan and men much, so that it might become apparent

---

15 Quoted in Hyma, *Albertus C. Van Raalte*, 39.
16 Quoted in Reenders, "Van Raalte," 297.
17 Cees Veenhof makes this same observation in *Prediking en uitverkiezing*, 5.
18 Van Gelderen makes this same point in *Simon van Velzen*, 31.

that the liberation and nurturing of the churches is *His* work, and whoever boasts, does not boast in De Cock or Scholte, Van Velzen or Brummelkamp, but only in the Lord."[19] Another minister wrote later, "And so it came to pass that, after a struggle of nearly fifty years, the Christian Reformed Church may say: by the grace of God I am what I am."[20]

19 Lucas Lindeboom, quoted in Veenhof, *Prediking en uitverkiezing*, 9.
20 Willem H. Gispen, quoted in Veenhof, *Prediking en uitverkiezing*, 11.

PART 4

PROFESSOR

(1854–96)

Chapter 11

———⟡———

A NEW BEGINNING

The year 1854 stands out as a significant milestone in the history of the Afscheiding churches as well as in the life of Van Velzen. First, this was the year that differences between Van Velzen and Brummelkamp were finally smoothed over, and second, this was the year that the theological school in Kampen was established.

Ever since 1840, two parties had formed within the denomination, and since 1847, the churches in Gelderland and Overijssel had been divided, with Brummelkamp and his followers largely isolating themselves from the fellowship of the other churches. This unhealthy situation festered for nearly a decade, consuming the time of the churches and sapping them of strength.

A national synod was held in 1849 in Amsterdam to try to bring about a resolution, but synod still judged that the Gelderse had rejected the Reformed principle that narrower assemblies must submit to the decisions of the broader assemblies. They judged the Gelderse to be too independent in their church polity by denying the binding authority of synodical decisions.

Several provincial synods were held in Gelderland and Overijssel in 1850 to address the issues. But now a new hurdle presented itself: Brummelkamp had made plans with men from the Hervormde Kerk, including men such as Isaac da Costa and Groen van Prinsterer, to collaborate on a new seminary in Amsterdam. A building had been purchased, curriculum had been prepared, students had been enrolled, and Brummelkamp had even bought a house in Amsterdam. But Brummelkamp eventually came to see that the seminary plans were preventing reunion talks because the Drentse were suspicious of his involvement with men from the state church, so he backed out of the arrangement.

Another national synod was held in 1851, again in Amsterdam, with Van Velzen chosen to serve as chairman. The result was largely the same as in 1849: synod was still concerned about the church political views of the Gelderse.

Finally, there was a breakthrough at a meeting of a provincial synod of the Drentse held in Zwolle on June 23–24, 1852. At that meeting, Brummelkamp was present as a representative of the Gelderse. Several doctrinal and church political questions were asked of the Gelderse, and the Drentse were satisfied with the answers. Among those questions were the following:

Q. 1: Faith is commanded, unbelief is sin, and to believe is our duty. Is man able to accept Christ in his own strength? A.: No, the picture of man in his unconverted state is Lazarus in the grave.

Q. 2: Does the essence of faith consist in an assured act of faith, or should we rather view assurance as a fruit of faith? A.: The Catechism rightly says in Lord's Day 7 that faith consists in knowledge and trust. The knowledge can be small and the trust can also be small.

Q. 5: Do you allow children to attend the Lord's Supper?

A.: No, not all children but only those who are converted and spiritually mature enough to discern the body of Christ. We do not go by personal feelings in this matter but we willingly submit to ecclesiastical direction.

Q. 6: Has Christ atoned for the sins of all men or only for the sins of His elect? A.: As far as actual salvation is concerned, Christ's satisfaction benefits only the elect. In that sense His satisfaction is restricted to those for whom He made intercession in John 17:9.

Q. 8: What is your view of the Secession? Did you secede from the Reformed Church as Association (Fellowship) or as Reformed Church Administration? A.: We separated ourselves from the Reformed Administration as it manifested itself since 1816 but not from the Reformed Church as it existed from the Reformation until 1816.

Q. 9: If and when we are reunited, how will you deal with the issue of the clerical dress for ministers? A.: The matter of how ministers should dress need not present an obstacle. In time it will be resolved in accordance with the needs of the various congregations.[1]

At a subsequent provincial synod of the Gelderse held in Arnhem on November 17, 1852, these decisions of the Drentse meeting were brought forward for ratification. Van Velzen was present and proposed three points of agreement for the Gelderse side to sign, which they agreed to do. From this point on, the two sides no longer held separate assemblies but were reunited.

---

1 Quoted in Pronk, *A Goodly Heritage*, 216–17. I've taken the liberty to re-number the questions according to the original found in Te Velde, *Anthony Brummelkamp*, 219–20.

However, the reunion of the two sides was not universally accepted. Joffers and a small minority of the Drentse still distrusted the Gelderse, and they brought these issues to the national synod of 1854. After deliberating on the matter, synod asked the Gelderse delegates to subscribe to the following:

> That in order for the reunion agreed upon in Zwolle and Arnhem to be ratified by Synod, we the undersigned, wishing to allay the fears of the brothers, declare that we are in good conscience united with God's Word, the Forms of Unity and the Church Order of 1619 and everything connected therewith…Regarding certain acts committed by us in which we may have sinned, we place ourselves completely in the hands of Synod and are ready to make confession of guilt if it can be shown on good grounds that some of us have acted wrongly in specific matters and that this meeting declares that such confessions will be made by both sides.[2]

Brummelkamp and the Gelderse agreed to do so, and the reunion was a reality. After the synod, Brummelkamp said:

> "Father," says the High priest of our confession, "I will that they all may be one, as thou, Father, art in me, and I in thee." Could his Spirit possibly live in us if we did not thirst after this unity? How can we not be deeply grieved at the breaking up of the body of Christ? If we ask what history has taught us in this regard, the answer is that it has been very easy for the Prince of Darkness to bring about schism after schism in the church and to cause brothers to take up arms against each other, making them

---

2   Quoted in Pronk, *A Goodly Heritage*, 218–19.

tear into and devour each other! And what about repairing the breaches? The greater the efforts to heal wounds, the greater was the despair each time the attempt failed. And since our experience of the past twenty years has confirmed to us the one as well as the other in a most powerful way, we ought to exclaim in adoration and amazement: "God hath done great things for us; whereof we are glad!" (Psalm 126:3).[3]

◆ ◆ ◆

The Synod of 1854 not only brought about the reunion of the two warring factions in the denomination, but it also marked the beginning of the seminary at Kampen. The establishment of the seminary was nearly twenty years in the making. The seed was planted early, but it took many years to germinate and strike down roots.

The two-decade delay was not due to a failure to see the need for trained ministers. This was apparent to all. Already at her birth the reformation had struggled because of a lack of qualified men. As more and more people left the mother church and more and more congregations joined the new denomination, the seceding congregations were served by only a handful of ministers. That number was reduced even further when the first synod deposed Rev. van Rhee.

Obviously they could not send their students to the liberal universities where Van Velzen and the other fathers had been trained. To think that they would even be accepted was laughable. But what were the churches to do?

One of the earliest proposed solutions to the problem was to

---

3   Quoted in Pronk, *A Goodly Heritage*, 219.

make use of oefenaars. A staple of the pious and often mystical conventicles of earlier years, these were unordained men who led small groups in worship by reading the Bible and the *oude schrijvers*. The thought of some was immediately to ordain these lay preachers and ease the burden on the already overburdened clergy.

The matter came up at the first synod, where it was supported by Hendrik de Cock. Despite the backing of this father, the proposal was rejected. This was due largely to Van Velzen, who was one of its most outspoken opponents. In a subsequent article in *De Reformatie*, Van Velzen argued that ordaining oefenaars would be unwise. None of the oefenaars had received seminary training, and some of them could not even write. He also questioned whether some of them were motivated by pride and a desire for a prominent place in the church. He said, "When *oefenaars* are given the pulpit to preach, it is not difficult to notice that pride and desire for honor soon come into play."[4] Above all, the simple fact was that they were not ordained and therefore not called by God to this work. If these lay preachers were employed, Van Velzen wrote, at the very least they ought not preach their own sermons, but merely read those written by ordained men.[5]

Van Velzen's argument carried the day, and the oefenaars were not ordained. Some, like Douwe Vander Werp, trained to become ordained ministers, while others stepped down and again assumed the role of elders in their local congregations.

---

4 Quoted in Heideman, *Hendrik P. Scholte*, 119.

5 Sheeres, *Son of Secession*, 54–55; Jacob E. Nyenhuis and George Harinck, eds., *The Enduring Legacy of Albertus C. Van Raalte as Leader and Liaison*, The Historical Series of the Reformed Church in America 81 (Grand Rapids, MI: William B. Eerdmans Publishing Co., 2014), 197–98. The reference is to Van Velzen's article "Brief van eenen leeraar aan de Christelijke Gereformeerde Gemeente in Nederland" ["Letter from a minister in the Christian Reformed Church in the Netherlands"], *De Reformatie*, 3:336–58.

With oefenaars rejected and the liberal universities out of the question, Van Velzen and the other leaders chose a middle course. While they laid the groundwork for a seminary, they would take interested men into the parsonage and provide them with private tutelage. Some men, such as elders or experienced oefenaars, needed little training and were finished in six months. Others, including young men with no previous ecclesiastical experience, needed longer and studied for three or four years.

The specific instruction obviously varied from manse to manse, but it generally consisted of the same subjects: Bible history, exegesis, dogmatics, church history, homiletics, and pastoral theology. The instruction in dogmatics was heavily dependent on Aegidius Francken's *Kern der Christelijke Leer* (*Kernel of Christian Doctrine*).

When a man was deemed sufficiently trained, he had to endure a grueling examination before a provincial synod. Besides preaching a specimen sermon, the students were examined in exegesis, dogmatics, church history, and apologetics (known to some as controversy). Van Velzen was not directly involved in the instruction of these candidates, but his part in the process came at this stage because he was almost always one of the denomination-ally-appointed examiners who traveled to each of the provincial gatherings to conduct the examinations.

Over time, four main centers of training were made available to men who felt the call of God to the ministry.

Two of the centers were in the northern part of the country. One was in the city of Groningen, where students were trained by Hendrik de Cock. Two of the first men to study under him were the brothers Frederick Alberts Kok and Wolter Alberts Kok (1805–91). From the time of the Secession until his death in 1842, De Cock trained twenty-seven men who were ordained into the ministry. After De Cock's death, Tamme Foppes de Haan stepped into this position.

Wolter Alberts Kok

Jan Bavinck

The other main center in the north was first located in Ruinerwold and then moved to Hoogeveen. The instructor there was W. A. Kok, who began teaching shortly after he was ordained in 1842. He was later assisted by Jan Bavinck (1826–1909), father of Herman Bavinck.

The other two main centers were in the south. One was the school of Scholte in Utrecht, and the other was in Arnhem, where Brummelkamp and Van Raalte collaborated.

The two "schools" in the north flourished. Of the 164 ministers ordained between 1839 and 1854, close to 75 percent of them were from the northern centers. In contrast, the training centers in the south struggled. The struggles of Scholte's school corresponded to Scholte's own ministerial struggles. The school in Arnhem struggled, in part because reportedly Brummelkamp was disorganized and Van Raalte was not very scholarly, and in part because Van Raalte emigrated to America in 1846.[6]

This private instruction was intended only as a stopgap measure. While this sit-

---

6 Te Velde, "The Dutch Background," in *Breaches and Bridges*, 86–87; Nyenhuis and Harinck, *Enduring Legacy of Albertus C. Van Raalte*, 208–9. Some argue that the instruction in Arnhem was better, e.g. Algra, *Het wonder van de 19e eeuw*, 154; Pronk, *A Goodly Heritage*, 203.

uation kept the churches free from the errors espoused at Leiden and its ilk, the arrangement was not ideal. For one thing, a number of the students came for training with very little formal education, some barely knowing how to read or write. Many of the students also worked during the day to make a living and were able to study only at night. Busy pastors were burdened with the additional work of training these aspirants, and the theological instruction they provided lacked uniformity. What is more, at times the instructors had very little previous education. W. A. Kok, for instance, was a farmer with no university education who received his training in the parsonage of De Cock, and who, when he was ordained, was immediately put in charge of training other men. Kok later recalled:

> What did I think of the task given me in this mandate? In my heart I had to laugh about myself. Not being a man of letters, and having enjoyed little education, I now had to train others! But I was also somewhat aware of the gift, that with the blessing of the Lord, I could make others wiser than I was myself. I started that professional work. The students came to me every week to get their lessons. Their number grew. They came from various provinces of our country…Every week they had to pay fl. 1.50 for meals and they received the instruction free. All in all, it was little, but we were allowed to experience the blessing of the Lord. We also received a teacher of languages, a certain Rozensweigh, who having been a Jew, had become a member of our church. Thereby the instruction was broadened and improved to a large extent.[7]

---

7   Quoted in Pronk, *A Goodly Heritage*, 205–6.

Helenius de Cock

In addition, the different training centers were indicative of the different parties in the churches, with each side suspicious about candidates from the opposite side. Helenius de Cock, who was a minister in the denomination at the time, later wrote:

The almost simultaneous education of future ministers by different instructors without mutual consultation and begun without combined strength had more than one drawback. It solidified the already existing differences and opened the door for those desiring to be trained for the ministry to approach those instructors whose views were the closest to their own.[8]

The leaders in the churches were not oblivious to these problems. The Synod of 1846 in Groningen made a beginning in consolidating the instruction by calling T. F. de Haan to take over all theological instruction in Groningen and Friesland.[9] Three years later, the issue came up again and the synod chose three men to serve as professors: George F. Gezelle Meerburg, T. F. de Haan, and Van Velzen. When it received word of this decision, the consistory of the church in Amsterdam objected to their pastor being nominated. It claimed that he was simply too important to their congregation for him to leave and teach in the seminary.

Despite these early efforts, no concrete solution materialized. The issue was finally resolved by the Synod of 1854 in Zwolle. On July 15, synod voted to establish their own seminary in the small

---

8   Quoted in Pronk, *A Goodly Heritage*, 207.
9   Sheeres, *Son of Secession*, 85. Wormser informs us that De Haan was especially gifted in Hebrew and Aramaic (*Karakter en genade*, 85).

town of Kampen. All the smaller training centers would close, and the students would come together at the new school. Rather than an independent body, the seminary would be an ecclesiastical institution supervised by a curatorium chosen from the churches.[10]

Out of a gross list of thirteen ministers,[11] four were to be chosen as the first professors. Van Velzen was chosen unanimously, as was T. F. de Haan. Notably, having just received Brummelkamp back into the fold, synod cemented the reunion by unanimously approving him as a third instructor. The fourth man chosen by synod was Jan Bavinck, father of Herman Bavinck, noted Dutch theologian and future professor at Kampen and the Free University in Amsterdam. After much agonizing soul-searching and indecision, Jan Bavinck wrote two letters: one accepting the appointment and the other declining it. He then had a student pick one of the envelopes. The student chose the decline letter. Helenius de Cock, son of Hendrik de Cock, was chosen in Bavinck's place.[12]

Van Velzen bade farewell to the congregation in Amsterdam on November 26, 1854. He preached two farewell sermons that

---

10 Cf. Barrett Gritters, "Who Will Train the Churches' Ministers?" *Standard Bearer* 91, no. 4 (November 15, 2014): 77–80.

11 The men were J. Bavinck, A. Brummelkamp, Hel. de Cock, P. Dijksterhuis, T. F. de Haan, G. W. van Houten, F. A. Kok, W. A. Kok, G. F. Gezelle Meerburg, P. J. Oggel, H. G. Poelman, D. Postma, and S. van Velzen. Cf. Achttiende Sessie, article 5 of *Handelingen van de Synode 1854* in *Handelingen en verslagen*, 613.

12 Wormser, *Karakter en genade*, 114–16; Negentiende Sessie, article 3 of *Handelingen van de Synode 1854* in *Handelingen en verslagen*, 614. Ron Gleason mistakenly says that Helenius de Cock was unanimously chosen on the first ballot by synod and that T. F. de Haan was not elected (*Bavinck*, 22–24). In actuality, De Haan was voted in on the first ballot while De Cock was chosen later, after Jan Bavinck declined the position.

day: one on Revelation 22:10b and the other on Ephesians 3:14–21. He had been their pastor for over fourteen years, but he now left to take up his work in Kampen.

Kampen was a relatively small town of only thirteen thousand residents at the time, much smaller than the nearby city of Zwolle. It was in a rural area along the Ijssel River. The new school was located along the Oudestraat, a cobblestoned street with a beautiful view of the river and under the shadow of the grand, steepled Boven Kerk.

With the other professors, Van Velzen became one of the ministers in the Kampen congregation, where he was considered part of the consistory and was allowed to sit in on and vote at all its meetings. He lived in a large house on the same street as the school (Oudestraat 41), directly across the street from Brummelkamp's house, and a little way down the street lived another brother-in-law, Carel de Moen, president of the curatorium.

The doors of the seminary at Kampen finally opened on December 6, 1854, with four professors and thirty-seven enrolled students.

Chapter 12

———— ⊷◈⊶ ————

THE PROFESSOR

*T*he beginning of Kampen was truly a day of small things. Classes were initially held in the homes of the professors. Later, the school moved to a nearby primary school, and in 1870, the curatorium bought the home of Helenius de Cock and renovated it into a permanent home for the school. The professors were not even permitted to take the title of professors, but were referred to merely as *docenten* ("lecturers").[1]

Students enrolled at Kampen could expect to spend, on average, six years in the classroom before being declared a candidate for the ministry in the churches. The curriculum was divided into two levels: a pre-seminary literary department and the regular theological department. Each department required three years of intense study. The literary department was necessary because many of the men who enrolled had not received a higher education.

The four professors chosen by synod were assigned courses in

———

1   The professors continued to be called *docenten* for the next twenty years or more, for the Synod of 1875 rejected a proposal to refer to the instructors as professors but retained the title of *docenten*. Cf. James Eglinton, *Bavinck: A Critical Biography* (Grand Rapids, MI: Baker Academic, 2020), 62.

both the literary and the theological departments. These assignments were based on the varying gifts and strengths of the men.

T. F. de Haan was chosen to teach philosophy and logic in the literary department. In the theological department, he was assigned the chair in dogmatics, where he leaned heavily on the works of Johannes à Marck and Aegidius Francken. Because of his renown as a linguist, De Haan was also selected to teach Greek, Hebrew, Syrian, Arabic, and Chaldean.

Brummelkamp taught Dutch, Latin, Greek, and Greek and Roman antiquities in the literary department. He was chosen to teach Old and New Testament exegesis, symbolics, liturgics, and church polity in the theological department.

(left to right: Tamme Foppes de Haan, Simon van Velzen, Anthony Brummelkamp, Helenius de Cock)

Helenius de Cock taught courses in Dutch, Latin, geography, and history in the literary department. In the theological department, he began by teaching Old and New Testament history and introduction to the Bible.

Van Velzen was chosen to teach French, Latin, Greek, and Hebrew in the literary department of the seminary. In the theological department, he was the professor of ethics, natural theology, and church history. Van Velzen was also the professor of preaching (i.e., homiletics), a position he held until 1891. In addition to these regular teaching responsibilities, he held the position of librarian and archivist for the churches and the theological school.[2]

In his position as lecturer in church history, Van Velzen instructed his students on the entire history of the New Testament church, from her earliest years up to the Afscheiding itself. But in his public writings, he devoted a large proportion of his time to defending the Secession and showing its place in the broader stream of church history.

In the eyes of some, this narrow perspective is an indication that Van Velzen's strengths were not in the area of church history. The claim is made that he did not do much in the way of independent research and did not contribute anything new and substantial to the corpus of church historical literature. Therefore, his influence in this area was necessarily limited.[3]

This was a criticism leveled against the theological school as a whole. Some judged that the instruction at Kampen did not meet scholarly expectations and the high standards of academia. As a young man, Herman Bavinck—himself a professor at Kampen in later years—shared this judgment. He wrote, "I spent one year at the Theol. School in Kampen, where my father was now a minister. But the education there did not satisfy me. So in 1874, I went to Leiden to study theology under the famous professors

---

2 Lammert Hulst mistakenly claims that Van Velzen was first chosen to teach dogmatics, but certain issues caused the curatorium to give this department to Helenius de Cock a few years after the start of the school (Lammert J. Hulst, *Drie en zestig jaren prediker: Gedenkschriften van Ds. Lammert J. Hulst* [Sixty-three years a preacher: Memoirs of Rev. Lammert J. Hulst] [Grand Rapids, MI: Eerdmans Sevensma, 1913], 23).

3 George Harinck, "The Secession of 1834 as Frame of Reference," in *Breaches and Bridges*, 141, 151n1.

Scholten and Kuenen."[4] Although Bavinck desired ordination in the churches of the Secession, he decided after one year of attending Kampen (1873–74) not to return. Instead, he studied under the liberal professors at Leiden because they were more "scientific" than the professors at Kampen. In contrast to the men at Kampen,

A younger
Herman Bavinck

the Leiden professors were widely published and internationally respected theologians.

Bavinck's decision caused a major stir in the denomination and among the seminary faculty. Brummelkamp in particular wanted to force Bavinck to return to Kampen. Van Velzen cautioned his colleague against taking that line. He argued that Bavinck's father might respond by latching on to the fact that Brummelkamp allowed Christians from other denominations to partake of the Lord's supper. If an exception was made for Brummelkamp's position on the Lord's supper, surely, Van Velzen reasoned, an exception could be made for Bavinck not attending Kampen. Apart from the details, this incident exposed some of the criticisms of the school.

Several explanations could be given for these supposedly low standards. This may have been because the professors never pursued any higher degrees. It may have been because these men were still busy building and guiding the relatively new denomination and were stretched far too thin. Additionally, the professors were more interested in training good preachers than in producing ivory-tower scholars, and many of the men who enrolled as students had little formal education.

◆ ◆ ◆

---

4   Quoted in Eglinton, *Bavinck*, 66.

Some questions might linger about Van Velzen's scholarly qualifications as a church historian, but no debate exists about his
abilities in the area of preaching and homiletics. In the eyes of
one historian, he was "the celebrated preacher of the Afscheiding"
and "the eminent homilete."[5] Van Velzen saw this instruction as
his primary task as professor, the most important service he could
give to the church. Rather than focusing his attention and efforts
on publishing works of church history and producing students
who were capable scholars, he devoted himself to preparing his
students to be capable preachers of the word.

One of his students later wrote of Van Velzen, "A beloved
subject for him was homiletics." In the last year of their training,
the men under Van Velzen's direction would conduct practice
preaching sessions. The student reminisces that:

> Everyone in turn had to deliver a sermon upon a text that
> had been given the previous week. This was first critiqued
> by the fellow students and then by the professor. He knew
> how to appreciate the good, correct the wrong, and show
> us how to fill in the missing. Then he gave his own sketch
> of the same text that we could use if we later preached on
> that text. I made use of those professorial sketches in my
> first years in the ministry and others did as well.[6]

This "eminent homilete" made an important contribution to
the way the rising generation of ministers in the churches of the
Afscheiding preached. Prior to the opening of Kampen and Van
Velzen's appointment as professor of preaching, many preachers followed the "analytical" or "Holland" method, referred to

---

5 Keizer, "*Een paar brieven van wijlen Prof. S. van Velzen*," 414.
6 Quoted in Van Gelderen, *Simon van Velzen*, 39–40.

by some as "the usual Dutch style of preaching." Betraying his bias, J. J. van Oosterzee refers to this method as a "dry, diffuse exposition of Scripture." He adds, "Instead of leading their flocks into the fresh pastures of the Word," ministers "preferred taking them to the dry thistle fields of philological exegesis." This method promoted the "needless labour of the most exact analysis of every single word of the text."[7] In short, the analytical method led to preaching that consisted for the most part of word studies.

Van Velzen's judgment of this method mirrored that of Van Oosterzee.[8] He regarded it as a dry, lifeless method of preaching. In its place he substituted the "synthetic" or "English" method. This was the method associated with Ewald Hollebeek (1719–96) and was often referred to as the "Hollebeek" method. During the course of his labors as professor at Leiden, Hollebeek "became convinced that preaching in [the] land stood in need of a great reformation…More emphatically than any one before him did he oppose all unnecessary verbal explanations, and insisted that the main contents of the discourse should be devoted to the unfolding of the ideas contained in the text."[9]

Van Velzen learned this method from two sources. First, he

---

7   J. J. van Oosterzee, *Practical Theology: A Manual for Theological Students,* trans. Maurice J. Evans (London: Hodder and Stoughton, 1878), 150, 146–47.

8   Van Velzen thought highly of Van Oosterzee, referring to him as "a genius." After Van Oosterzee's *Praktische theologie* was published in 1877, it became the standard text at Kampen. In Van Velzen's opinion, it was a "priceless work." Cf. Trimp, "*S. van Velzen als prediker en homileet,*" 224, 239n6.

9   Van Oosterzee, *Practical Theology,* 150.

was taught this method at Leiden from his distinguished professor Johannes Clarisse. Second, this method was modeled for him by Lucas Egeling, the minister under whose preaching he sat during his seminary days at Leiden.

Van Velzen had the highest respect for the scriptures as the inspired word of God. In his work, he recognized a distinction between exegeting that word and preaching that word. Exegesis is the necessary foundation for preaching, but preaching must not devolve into a simple presentation of word etymologies and a dry analysis of sentence structures. Rather, preaching must be the explanation and application of the text in a lively manner.[10] In a letter to Helenius de Cock, Van Velzen wrote, "You...have received gifts from the Lord. Clearly and understandably...is the gospel proclaimed by you." In the same letter, Van Velzen addresses an apparent need in the denomination: "Conciseness and clarity in the preaching of the gospel is an element which our Afscheiding congregations need."[11]

Such preaching, in Van Velzen's judgment, must be done with boldness. This confidence was something he modeled for his students in his own preaching and was also something that he taught them in the classroom. In his rectoral address given in 1882, Van Velzen said:

> Courage is the soul of the preaching. Courage gives power and strength to the preaching; it shows the authority and the majesty of the Word. If, on the contrary, one is a preacher without courage, he on his part hinders the influence of the admonitions, the proper judgment of

---

10 Cf. Trimp's article "*S. van Velzen als prediker en homileet*," for more on Van Velzen's method.

11 Quoted in Keizer, "*Een paar brieven van wijlen Prof. S. van Velzen*," 413–14.

the matters, and the most penetrating conception. This scandalous weakness humiliates the ministry, causes the hearers to hold the ministry in contempt, shamelessly to reject the yoke of the Lord, and arrogantly to look down on the ministers.[12]

◆ ◆ ◆

Van Velzen was well respected, even beloved, by his students as a gifted teacher and caring mentor. Interestingly, one historian notes that, once they got to know him, Van Velzen's students found him to have "an easy, humorous personality."[13] A student later wrote of him:

> As a man he had a stern appearance, being on the grumpy side, but behind that stiff face he possessed a soft, tender heart. He was so kind-hearted and possessed a righteous character...As far as his dealings with the students are concerned, it may be testified that he always lived on very friendly terms. He loved the students very much, and the students loved him. No one would have ever dared to displease him. Without distinction people accorded him much esteem, love, and appreciation. It was wealth for his heart to be among his students.[14]

---

12 Quoted in David J. Engelsma, "The Courage of the Minister of the Word (concl.)," *Standard Bearer* 84, no. 21 (September 15, 2008): 490.

13 W. De Graaf, *Een monument der Afscheiding: De Theologische Hogeschool van de Gereformeerde Kerken in Nederland 1854–1954* [A monument of the Secession: The Theological School of the Reformed Churches in the Netherlands, 1854–1954] (Kampen: J. H. Kok, 1955), 57.

14 Quoted in Wormser, *Karakter en genade*, 164.

Another student, W. S. Veltman, who studied under Van Velzen from 1863 to 1868, referred to him as "the excellent Van Velzen." He said:

Beautiful shiny, very dark hair adorns his skull. Only a small bald spot is visible on the head. The most striking thing about Van Velzen are the eyes and the mouth. Those eyes twinkle. There is soul, there is life in them. A smile plays around the mouth. A good-hearted man and yet you get the impression that he knows what he wants. Many good things others have told me about him. He is able to preach excellently, have a beautiful presentation, and proclaim the truth very clearly and without any reservation. He also prayed fervently; that prayer has taken hold of me.[15]

Still another student, H. A. Dijkstra, who studied at Kampen from 1874 to 1882, referred to him as "the staunch Van Velzen." He wrote:

He was a knight without fear. This came out especially when he had to defend the honor of God. Then he proved to be a staunch Calvinist, who knew no turning back. By defending the sovereignty of God he inspired his students and this benefited the churches, because now the Reformed doctrine was clearly brought to the people, without a drop of strange blood in her veins. Much of the thanks goes to him that the churches of 1834 maintained the Reformed course, without deviating to the right or left.[16]

◆ ◆ ◆

---

15 Quoted in Van Gelderen, *Simon van Velzen*, 36.
16 Quoted in Van Gelderen, *Simon van Velzen*, 38–42.

Despite the progress made in unifying the two different parties in the churches, evidenced by the founding of Kampen in 1854, differences still lingered. These differences manifested themselves in the early years of seminary instruction.

The problems were due in large part to the fact that both professors and students were divided roughly in half, with one-half leaning in the direction of the Drentse richting and the other in the direction of the Gelderse richting. De Haan was firmly entrenched in the Drentse richting, and Van Velzen was often associated with that party. On the other side, Brummelkamp was firmly entrenched in the Gelderse richting, the party with which De Cock was often associated. The students also were divided. Of the nearly forty students who enrolled that first year, exactly half came with Brummelkamp from his school in Arnhem. The other half were from the schools in the north that belonged to the Drentse richting. Although a compromise had been hammered out at the Synod of 1854, nevertheless there were bound to be disagreements when these differing mindsets were thrown together.

For example, disagreements arose almost immediately between De Haan and Brummelkamp. De Haan was irritated that Brummelkamp seemed to think so highly of the students that he brought with him from Arnhem and so poorly of the students from the north. He was also disgruntled with Brummelkamp's taking it upon himself to invite the northern students to his home in order to evaluate them. Brummelkamp fired back that De Haan was being unnecessarily old-fashioned and stiff in his instruction.

The sentiments of the professors were likewise shared by their protégés. The students who agreed with De Haan were critical of Brummelkamp, citing doctrinal errors in his exegesis of such passages as John 3:16, as well as deficiencies in his preaching. The students who sided with Brummelkamp in turn excoriated De Haan. They objected to the instruction given in his dogmatics lectures and especially bristled at his use of Aegidius Francken's work of dogmatics. They also thought him to be a rather poor preacher.

The curators of the school did not have their heads in the sand. They were aware of the differences in the school and were laboring with both professors and students to bring some semblance of order and peace. But, it was becoming apparent to them that the most questionable students were those who adhered most closely to Brummelkamp. He seemed to have a shadowy influence on some of the students.

A mere three years after the school's christening, the issues plaguing her were brought before the broadest ecclesiastical assembly for adjudication. Meeting in Leiden, the Synod of 1857 faced a number of objections to the instruction of Brummelkamp. Amid all the blustering and debate, Van Velzen appeared with a proposed resolution to bring about the desired unity and peace. He presented eight doctrinal points to which all four professors must agree. If they agreed, no further questioning of their orthodoxy would be tolerated. The eight doctrinal points regarded the innate knowledge of God, the eternal generation of the Son, Adam's sin and the covenant of works, four distinct kinds of faith, the internal calling, baptism and children, the church, and particular atonement. The resolution was adopted by the synod, and it appeared that unity had finally been achieved.

Such was not to be the case, however. De Haan's objections against his colleagues seemed to increase after the resolution of the synod. In 1858, De Haan presented the curators with a list of grievances against not only Brummelkamp but also Van Velzen. He criticized Van Velzen for using new works of dogmatics and for his new method of preaching that rejected the old, analytical method. He also was bitter that Van Velzen snookered the best teaching hours. At their meeting on June 2 of that year, the curators received a notice from Brummelkamp. So fed up was he with the way things were going that he offered to resign from his post and go back into the active ministry. The curators declined. Things continued to grow worse over the following year. At a meeting in October 1858, the situation had gotten so bad that Van Velzen suggested to the curatorium that they recommend to the next synod that synod replace all four professors and call four new ones. The curators again declined.

It was becoming more and more apparent to all involved that De Haan was largely responsible for the problems the school was facing. Not only had he adopted a warlike attitude toward his colleagues, but he was also beginning to show the effects of his advancing age (he was sixty-nine years old). With this in mind, the curators recommended to the Synod of 1860, meeting in Hoogeveen, that De Haan be declared emeritus. Synod concurred, and De Haan was officially relieved of his duties on September 1. No new professor was called to replace him, but the remaining three men were asked to pick up the slack by taking the courses that De Haan had taught.

In a significant move, the synod appointed De Cock to replace De Haan as chair of dogmatics. This decision raises the question: why was Van Velzen not chosen to fill this opening? He was, after all, regarded as the preeminent theologian of the churches. Veenhof's answer is that the delegates did not want to alienate the Brummelkampian party and widen the breach between the two by appointing Van Velzen to this important position. Instead, they chose De Cock, a young man from outside of the group, to fill the chair and keep the peace.[17]

The year 1860 did not put an end to all disagreement in the churches. The following chapter will document further arguments. However, this year did bring about a level of peace and cooperation almost unheard-of in the churches of the Afscheiding to this point in her history.

---

17 Veenhof, *Prediking en uitverkiezing*, 89.

Chapter 13

WAR AND PEACE

*T*he decades of the 1860s and 1870s were an interesting mixture of internal controversy and outward-looking ecumenism in the Secession churches, and Van Velzen demonstrated his leadership throughout. This period therefore gives insight into two significant aspects of Van Velzen's personality: he was a warrior who fought uncompromisingly for the truth when necessary, but he was also a peace-loving man who treasured the unity of the church and sought to express it as much as possible.

Although a certain measure of peace had been reached in the churches of the Secession with the founding of Kampen, this by no means meant that all disputes were finished. A number of issues arose, and Van Velzen was called upon to help settle them all.

One issue that continued to crop up at this time was the matter of the well-meant offer of the gospel. This had been one of the underlying causes for the existence of the two parties in the church during the 1840s, and some continued to hold nagging suspicions about Brummelkamp's orthodoxy on this matter. In fact, a protest was lodged with the Synod of Leiden in 1857 against Brummelkamp's preaching of the well-meant offer. Although synod took no action against him, it did feel the need to declare that the Reformed confessions "rejected universal atonement," an idea implied in Brummelkamp's teaching.[1]

Another outspoken defender of the well-meant offer at this time was Jan R. Kreulen (1820–1904), minister in Hallum, Friesland.[2] Kreulen claimed that in the  preaching there is a "well-meant offer of the grace of God in Christ to all who live under the gospel, with the purpose that they all would accept and obtain possession of that salvation, only on the ground of that offer which comes to them as sinners."[3] He claimed that this well-meant offer is "a declaration made by the truthful and holy God and that he earnestly, truthfully, and well-meaningly goes out offering his grace in Christ to all who live under the preaching of the gospel, without deceit, insincerity, and dissembling."[4]

Jan R. Kreulen

Van Velzen opposed this position vehemently. Writing in the church magazine *De Bazuin* (*The Trumpet*) in 1858, Van Velzen noted, "It is the great question upon which everything

---

1 Article 69 of *Handelingen van de Synode 1857* in *Handelingen en verslagen*, 684. Quoted in Engelsma, "Covenant Doctrine," in *Always Reforming*, 106.

2 Kreulen had a strong doctrinal influence on Lammert J. Hulst (1825–1922) while the latter was minister in the neighboring village of Ferwerd. Hulst later immigrated to the United States and became an important figure in the Christian Reformed Church. Cf. Hulst, *Drie en zestig jaren prediker*, 56–65; Jelle Faber, *American Secession Theologians on Covenant and Baptism* (Neerlandia, Alberta: Inheritance Publications, 1996), 19.

3 Veenhof, *Prediking en uitverkiezing*, 46. Quoted in David J. Engelsma, *Hyper-Calvinism and the Call of the Gospel: An Examination of the "Well-Meant Offer" of the Gospel*, 3rd ed. (Jenison, MI: Reformed Free Publishing Association, 2014), 99.

4 Veenhof, *Prediking en uitverkiezing*, 47. Quoted in Engelsma, *Hyper-Calvinism*, 99.

here depends, 'What does one understand by the general offer?'"[5]
He asked, "Does the word 'offer' then mean that God promises to bestow grace and salvation upon all who come under the
preaching of the gospel?" Van Velzen's answer was emphatic:
"Absolutely not!" He then explained how the word is to be prop-
erly understood:

> We learned that God promises rest of soul and eternal life
> to all who come to Him and believe, not to all who come
> under the preaching of the gospel...(The offer of Christ
> in the gospel means) that Christ is proclaimed in the gos-
> pel as the only, all-sufficient Savior, and thus as the only
> object of faith in order to be able rightly to know Him,
> and in order to take refuge in Him unto salvation. This
> proclamation must go out to all men.[6]

Van Velzen continued:

> But if one adds to this, "and that he promises to all to
> whom the gospel's doctrine of salvation is preached, to
> bestow (on them) grace and salvation," then surely no
> one who has some little esteem for the word of God can
> agree with such an opinion even in the slightest. What?
> God promises to all to whom the gospel's doctrine of sal-
> vation is preached, that he shall bestow (on them) grace
> and salvation? He would thus promise and not fulfill
> his promise, as we see the evidence in numberless per-
> sons who remain unconverted under the preaching. This

---

5   Veenhof, *Prediking en uitverkiezing*, 54. Quoted in Engelsma, *Hyper-Calvinism*, 100.
6   Veenhof, *Prediking en uitverkiezing*, 55–56. Quoted in Nelson D. Kloosterman, "The Doctrinal Significance of the Secession of 1834," in *The
Reformation of 1834*, 40.

opinion is denial of God's truth. Nothing more about this needs to be said.[7]

Despite Van Velzen's response to Kreulen's claim, the differences in the churches regarding the well-meant offer of the gospel were never settled and continued to linger. What is noteworthy is that the denial of the well-meant offer is found in the Reformed tradition. At times, the idea is expressed in Reformed circles today that the promotion of the well-meant offer is the only Reformed position. That is not true. There is ample evidence, including the powerful influence of a man like Van Velzen, that the denial of the well-meant offer is well established in the Reformed tradition.

◆ ◆ ◆

Van Velzen was involved in another, different—albeit intimately related—doctrinal dispute during his years at Kampen. This time, the controversy focused on the doctrine of the covenant of grace.[8]

In 1861, Kreulen and Klaas J. Pieters, minister at the time in Franeker, Friesland,[9] wrote a work entitled *De kinderdoop* (*Infant*

---

7   Veenhof, *Prediking en uitverkiezing*, 54–55. Quoted in Engelsma, *Hyper-Calvinism*, 101.

8   For a more in-depth treatment of this controversy, cf. Engelsma, "Covenant Doctrine," in *Always Reforming*, 100–36; and Engelsma, *Covenant and Election*, 9–14.

9   Later, Klaas Pieters became ensnared in alcohol abuse, was removed from the ministry in Franeker, and left the CGK altogether for the Free Evangelical Church. Cf. Gleason, *Bavinck*, 72–73. Herman Bavinck, who later served as pastor of the congregation in Franeker, said of Pieters, "For a few years, there was a minister here who was certainly an exception in the whole of our church. Unusually sharp in intellect, he could not be satisfied with our confession, didn't bother himself with it, and preached what he himself found good. Alongside this, he was guilty of a very great misuse of strong drink—all of this together meant he was eventually deposed. My predecessor, Eskes, had much conflict with the friends of this

Baptism)[10] in which they introduced into the churches the doctrine of a conditional covenant. An important element of their teaching was their defense of a covenant that is cut loose from election. Pieters and Kreulen wrote, "Let us then regarding Baptism forget about eternal election and establish that the promise of the covenant is bestowed and offered as the revealed counsel of God and refers to every baptized [child] in the visible church without any exception."[11]

In keeping with this view, Pieters and Kreulen also defended the notion of conditions in the covenant. After all, if the covenant is established with every single baptized child, what accounts for the fact that not all baptized children are saved? The answer is some of the baptized children failed to meet the necessary conditions. The two ministers said, "The cause why this is the case [namely, that the covenant promises go unfulfilled most of the time] must absolutely not be sought in this, as if on God's part the promises were given to the one and not to the other.

---

deposed minister. And there are still those who condemn the sin of the former minister Pieters, but still entertain his doctrine. From that, there is here—which in our church otherwise never arises—much confusion and difference of opinions. In particular, Pieters's faithful followers are quite prominent and imagine and regard themselves to be quite clever. So far, however, they have been satisfied by my preaching. Particularly when I disapprove of their feelings, I try, through conversations here and there, to correct them. A lot can be done with patience and love." Quoted in Eglinton, *Bavinck*, 122.

10 The full title is *De kinderkoop volgens de beginselen der Gereformeerde Kerk in hare gronden, toedieningen en praktijk* (Infant baptism according to the principles of the Reformed Church in its grounds, administrations, and practice) (Franeker: T. Telenga, 1861).

11 Pieters and Kreulen, *De kinderkoop volgens de beginselen der Gereformeerde Kerk in hare gronden, toedieningen en praktijk*, 48. Quoted in Engelsma, "Covenant Doctrine," in *Always Reforming*, 109.

But the cause is found in this, that the divine promises are not given, signified, and sealed unconditionally in Baptism."[12]

The view of the covenant defended by Pieters and Kreulen was never officially rejected by the churches of the Afscheiding. A protest against their teaching was lodged with the Synod of Franeker in 1863. Synod made clear that it did not think the covenant conception of the two ministers was "in all respects the most correct expression of the sentiments of the Reformed Church."[13] Despite its misgivings, synod nevertheless rejected the protest on the table and declared that it was "not able to condemn the brothers [Pieters and Kreulen] as being in conflict with the confessions of the Church."[14] The judgment of the synod was that the confessions did not specifically address the covenant, and therefore different views could be held.

Van Velzen was present at that meeting of synod in an advisory role. He disapproved of the decision and made sure that his objection to it was recorded in the minutes.[15] This is not surprising, because Van Velzen had already made his view on this matter clear several years before. At the Synod of Leiden in 1857, besides dealing with the issue of the well-meant offer in the preaching of Brummelkamp, Van Velzen was also compelled to answer his brother-in-law's position on the covenant.

E. Smilde summarizes Van Velzen's position in 1857 on cove-

---

12 Pieters and Kreulen, *De kinderkoop volgens de beginselen der Gereformeerde Kerk in hare gronden, toedieningen en praktijk*, 48. Quoted in Engelsma, "Covenant Doctrine," in *Always Reforming*, 112.

13 Engelsma, "Covenant Doctrine," in *Always Reforming*, 128.

14 Article 26 of *Handelingen van de Synode 1863* in *Handelingen en verslagen*, 829–30. Quoted in Engelsma, "Covenant Doctrine," in *Always Reforming*, 128.

15 Article 26 of *Handelingen van de Synode 1863* in *Handelingen en verslagen*, 829–30; Engelsma, "Covenant Doctrine," in *Always Reforming*, 128.

nant and election thus: "Van Velzen, on the basis of Rom. 9, held to the close connection between the covenant of grace and *election...*The two are not to be separated in his opinion. This is not surprising to us. It is well-known that he held firmly to the truth of election." Van Velzen also "strongly denied—with appeal to Rom. 9—that in the much-discussed expression of the first question for baptism ['sanctified in Christ'] it is certain that all children *head for head* will inherit salvation. Rather, the form speaks in the first question not of some child in particular but of our children generally." Smilde adds, "After an appeal to *the judgment of charity* with respect to adult believers, [Van Velzen] writes: So also do we hold the children of believers as sanctified in Christ, until the contrary is seen from their conduct."[16]

In response to Pieters and Kreulen, Van Velzen again conveyed his objections in writing in the pages of *De Bazuin*. He condemned the covenantal conception of his two colleagues, and in its place he taught an unconditional covenant with the children of believers, a covenant governed by God's sovereign decree of election. He wrote:

> The covenant of grace and our covenant relation with God in Christ have their origin and their ground in this covenant of redemption between God and Christ. From this proceeds the beginning, continuance, and end of the salvation of men. Before one existed, before the gospel was preached to him, it was already decreed and arranged in this covenant when he would be born, when and by what means he would be delivered [from sin], how much

---

16 Smilde, *Een eeuw van strijd over verbond en doop*, 31–32. Emphasis is Smilde's. Smilde refers to two articles written by Van Velzen in *De Bazuin* on August 7 and 14, 1857.

grace, comfort, and holiness, how much and what kind
of strife and cross he would have in this life—all of this
was decreed and comes to each one from this covenant.
The elect have then, on the one hand, to do nothing
and let the Lord work...By the power of this covenant,
the Lord Jesus is the one who carried out the salvation
of the elect.[17]

Later in the same article, Van Velzen wrote:

Here a matchless love reveals itself, which surpasses all
understanding. In this covenant [of redemption in eter-
nity], to be known and thought of; to be given by the
Father to the Son; to be written by the Son in His book;
to be an object of the eternal, mutual delight between the
Father and Christ to save you—that is blessedness! that is
a wonder! Here was no foreseen faith, no good works, by
which the parties were moved to think of certain persons
in this covenant. Here was no necessity, no constraint,
but only eternal love and sovereignty. "Yea, I have loved
thee with an everlasting love" (Jer. 31:3).[18]

In a subsequent issue of *De Bazuin*, Van Velzen concluded
his objections with these words: "It is easy to perceive that this
opinion [of a conditional covenant] must have great influence
on the preaching and that by necessary logical consequence the
idea of the covenant of redemption, election and reprobation,

---

17 Simon van Velzen, "Het verbond der verlossing" ("The covenant of redemption"), *De Bazuin* (January 20, 1865). Quoted in Engelsma, "Covenant Doctrine," in *Always Reforming*, 117.
18 Van Velzen, "Het verbond der verlossing." Quoted in Engelsma, "Covenant Doctrine," in *Always Reforming*, 118.

limited atonement, and such truths [the doctrines of grace as confessed in the Canons of Dordt] must undergo enormous change."[19]

One might wish that this issue had been resolved at this point. Instead, the differences were allowed to fester in the churches of the Afscheiding and would continue to cause problems years down the road. These differences can be seen in the Christian Reformed Church of the 1920s, with William Heyns advocating a conditional covenant and Herman Hoeksema defending an unconditional covenant. These differences can be seen in the formation of the Liberated Churches in the Netherlands under Klaas Schilder in the 1940s. And these differences can be seen in the split that rocked the Protestant Reformed Churches in the 1950s. In the providence of God, the Secession churches were not ready in the 1860s to settle the issue. Only in later decades and through painful controversy was the church's understanding on the doctrine of the covenant sharpened.

It is worth noting here, as before with the matter of the well-meant offer, that the denial of a conditional covenant is firmly entrenched in the Reformed tradition. It is not the case that the teaching of a conditional covenant is the only Reformed position. Rather, it can be argued that the preeminent theologians in the Reformed tradition rejected this in favor of an unconditional covenant. For instance, the view of Van Velzen regarding the covenant was similar in many respect to the views

---

19 Van Velzen, editorial comments on K. J. Pieters, "Eenige opmerkingen over de 69e vr. en antw. van den Katechismus" ("Some remarks on the 69th question and answer of the Catechism"), *De Bazuin* (May 19, 1865). Quoted in Engelsma, "Covenant Doctrine," in *Always Reforming*, 121.

later advocated by Abraham Kuyper,[20] Herman Bavinck,[21] and Herman Hoeksema.

◆ ◆ ◆

At the same time Van Velzen and other leaders were debating important matters of doctrine, they were also striving faithfully to manifest the unity of the church as much as they were able.

One way in which this was evident was in their attempt to bring about a reunion with the Kruisgezinden.[22] This was the separate denomination that had broken off when the Secession churches had failed to support the Church Order of Dordt as well as to approve the use of lay preachers (oefenaars). Their members were also incensed that the Secession churches had seemed so willing to relinquish their claim to the name *Gereformeerde* in order to gain government approval.

After several decades had passed, both sides began to realize that with changing circumstances they were now agreed on the points that had previously divided them. The two sides not only maintained the three forms of unity as their doctrinal basis, but the Secession churches had also reverted back to the Church Order of Dordt, which was held in high esteem by the Kruisgezinden. In addition, with the end of persecution and the approval of the government, the Secession churches were committed to

---

20 Veenhof says, "Van Velzen was not that far from Kuyper in his conception of the covenant and baptism" (*Prediking en uitverkiezing*, 136).

21 David Engelsma says, "The covenant doctrine of the fathers of the Secession [including Van Velzen] has always been maintained in the Reformed churches of the Dutch tradition. That it remained the dominant view in the Dutch Reformed churches standing in the tradition of the Secession is plain from Herman Bavinck's treatment of the covenant in his *Reformed Dogmatics*" ("Covenant Doctrine," in *Always Reforming*, 127).

22 The following information on reunion with the Kruisgezinden comes from Wormser, *Karakter en genade*, 133–46.

using the name *Gereformeerde*. Still, one of the major hangups was whether the Secession churches would recognize the ministers of the Kruisgezinden, since at the beginning of their history they had essentially ordained themselves.

Many meetings were held between the two parties, with Van Velzen leading the way in seeking to bring about a reconciliation. Work began already in 1849 in trying to iron out the differences. The Secession Synod of 1849 addressed a word of rebuke to the Kruisgezinden for leaving so many years before:

> Your behavior and ecclesiastical position are directly in conflict with God's Word, our Forms of Unity, as well as with our liturgy and Church Order. For this reason we must declare with sadness that you have rendered yourselves guilty of public schism, intrusion upon the holy ministry and profanation of the sacraments, while increasing your guilt as long as you continue in this way. Therefore we are not allowed to unite with you, lest we bring upon ourselves the Lord's displeasure. But we pray and advise you to confess your sins before the Lord and before men, fearing Him, for with the Lord there is forgiveness. Return to the communion of the church in order that we may rejoice with you and because of you.[23]

However, the next synod, in 1851, adopted a different tone toward the Kruisgezinden. Synod declared that it was prepared to leave the manner of the ordination of the Kruisgezinden ministers to the consciences of those churches. The synod also expressed grief that "so many years had already been spent in alienation from one another."[24]

---

23 Quoted in Pronk, *A Goodly Heritage*, 291.
24 Quoted in Pronk, *A Goodly Heritage*, 291.

Although progress was made, reunion did not take place immediately. The Secession churches were still concerned about the Kruisgezinden ministers being lawfully ordained, as well as the legitimacy of baptisms performed by them.

The Secession churches in the end agreed to recognize these ministers as lawfully ordained, and it was at the Synod of 1869 that the Kruisgezinden were finally restored to the fold. With the union of these two groups, the denomination now took the official name *Christelijke Gereformeerde Kerk* (Christian Reformed Church). According to Van Velzen, "I have attended all the Synods held by us in the thirty-three years since our exit from the Hervormde Church, but I can testify that in no such meetings has a more brotherly tone prevailed than here."[25]

Synod of 1869

Not all the Kruisgezinden were in favor of rejoining the CGK, however. Initially, three Kruisgezinden congregations refused to join and remained as an independent denomination, and this small group slowly grew over time. In 1907, through the work of Rev. G. H. Kersten, this group joined with a group of churches that had followed Rev. Lambertus Ledeboer—as well as several other small, independent groups—to form the *Gereformeerde Gemeenten in Nederland* (Reformed Congregations in the

---

25 Quoted in Wormser, *Karakter en genade*, 146.

Netherlands). This denomination is the mother of the Netherlands Reformed Congregations in America.

◆ ◆ ◆

The churches in the Netherlands also began reaching out to churches in other lands. One such example was the United Presbyterian Church of Scotland. In 1859, Van Velzen and Brummelkamp were sent as visiting delegates to the synod of that denomination. Van Velzen was delegated again in 1876.

Synod of 1879

At the same time, contact was established with the fledgling Christian Reformed Church in America (CRC). Van Raalte had left with a group for America in 1846, and he founded a colony near Holland, Michigan. At first, shortly after their arrival, the struggling churches of Classis Holland had decided to join the Reformed Church in America (RCA). However, they did so without a thorough knowledge of the RCA. By the spring of 1857, a group had left Classis Holland of the RCA and formed the CRC.

After their formation, the fledgling CRC reached out to the Secession churches to establish an official relationship and to find support. Van Velzen was largely supportive of this new group. When, for example, in 1873 a former student asked advice on a call to a CRC congregation, Van Velzen said, "I'd rather go to the True Holland Reformed Church [the CRC] than to the Reformed [the RCA]."[26] But, he was in the minority. Brummelkamp and many others were not ready to acknowledge this new denomination. Brummelkamp had told that same student, "I prefer to go to the [RCA]."[27] Part of the reason for this was the fact that Albertus van Raalte had decided to remain in the RCA, and he still carried significant influence among the leadership in the Secession churches. Many thought the CRC members were too rash in starting their own denomination and should have remained in the RCA. The effect of this was that the immigrants leaving the Secession churches for America were directed to affiliate with Van Raalte and the RCA, thus stifling the growth of the CRC.

The situation changed in 1882. At that time, the RCA was convulsed by a controversy over Freemasonry and lodge membership. The end result was that the RCA put its stamp of approval on lodge membership, a position that was anathema to the Dutch. From that point onward, the Secession churches recognized the CRC and encouraged their members who were moving to America to join her. With the forming of this relationship and the influx of immigrants, the CRC became well-established and grew by leaps and bounds.

Van Velzen obviously had a concern for the church of Christ beyond the walls of his own denomination. In his biography

---

26 Quoted in G. K. Hemkes, ed., *Een man des volks: Het leven van Prof. Geert Egberts Boer naar aanteekeningen uit zijn dagboek* [A man of the people: the life of Prof. Geert Egberts Boer according to notes out of his diary] (Grand Rapids, MI: J. B. Hulst, 1904), 77–78.

27 Quoted in Hemkes, *Een man des volks*, 77–78.

of H. P. Scholte, Lubbertus Oostendorp mistakenly wrote that Scholte's background "lent a broad, international, inter-denominational touch so obviously missing in De Cock and Van Velzen."[28] Such a statement does not harmonize with the facts, however. Van Velzen was interested in other churches and denominations. John Kromminga was correct when he wrote, "Furthermore, he [Van Velzen] emerges as a consistent and fervent proponent of a sort of ecumenicity."[29] Van Velzen was not the narrow-minded man he is so often portrayed to be.

---

28 Oostendorp, *H. P. Scholte*, 21.
29 John H. Kromminga, "'De Afscheiding'—Review and Evaluation," *Calvin Theological Journal* 20, no. 1 (April 1985): 48.

Chapter 14

UNION

On May 8, 1872, Van Velzen found himself in the sad and lonely, although familiar, position of being a widower. On that date, his third wife, Zwaantje, died. Van Velzen was sixty-two years old at the time. He would never marry again but would live out the remaining two decades of his life alone in Kampen.

Always devoted to his seminary students, Van Velzen poured himself into his teaching even more in the years that followed the passing of his wife. For instance, he issued a standing invitation for the students to come to his house on Sunday evenings, where they could engage in good theological discussions as well as light-hearted banter.

One student recalled, "He was also very fond of students coming to visit him on Sunday evenings. Then the pipes came out, and in no time no one could be seen anymore because of the clouds of smoke in which all were enveloped. At ten o'clock a psalm had to be sung and they went home in a happy mood."[1]

Another student, W. W. Smitt, also reminisced on memorable Sundays spent visiting "Van Velzen's large house," when they would fill the house with pipe smoke. Even in his old age, Van

---

1   Quoted in Wormser, *Karakter en genade*, 164.

Velzen "wore his gray head like a crown. He was fresh and green in his old days. He was always cheerful and ready to jest." The students "drank the instructive memories of the old man." Smitt concluded, "With all his quirks, the students truly loved him. He was a brother to the brethren. And everyone was aware that he intended the good of all."[2]

In spite of Van Velzen's great ability and the love of the students for him, the churches recognized that his increasing age would eventually catch up with him and hinder him from doing the work of the seminary at the same level as he was used to. A changing of the guard therefore took place at the Synod of 1882. At that synod, three new professors were appointed in order to begin transitioning out the three oldest professors (Van Velzen, Brummelkamp, and Helenius de Cock). Douwe Klazes Wielenga (1841–1902) was appointed to teach church history and church polity,[3] Lucas Lindeboom (1845–1933) was appointed to teach New Testament studies,[4] and Herman Bavinck was appointed to teach Reformed dogmatics and ethics. Bavinck also took over Van Velzen's duties as librarian and archivist of the school and denomination.

---

2   Quoted in Van Gelderen, *Simon van Velzen*, 42–44.

3   Wielenga had previously served pastorates in Oldehove (1864–67), Amsterdam (1867–73), and Nieuwendijk (1873–82). He and his second wife had six sons, all of whom became Reformed ministers or missionaries: Gerrit Wielenga (1872–1924), Bastiaan Wielenga (1873–1949), Jenne Johannes Wielenga (1874–1951), Douwe Klaas Wielenga (1880–1942), Johannes Dirk Wielenga (1881–1938), and Cornelis Jacobus Wielenga (1885–1964). He and Bavinck were good friends.

4   Lindeboom had previously served pastorates in 's-Hertogenbosch (1866–73) and Zaandam (1873–83). He and Bavinck would become fierce opponents of each other.

Douwe Klazes Wielenga   Lucas Lindeboom   Herman Bavinck

Although at seventy-three years old he was now relieved of most of his teaching responsibilities, Van Velzen maintained one important responsibility. He was still in charge of instructing the students in preaching, especially through practice preaching sessions. This was always his great love and where he excelled, and in this position he continued to shape young preachers.

Finally, in 1891, when he was eighty-two years old, Van Velzen was unable to continue teaching, and he became fully emeritus.

But, the Lord still had one more monumental work for Van Velzen to do before leaving the church militant.

◆ ◆ ◆

That great work was to bring about a union between the churches of the Afscheiding and the Doleantie.[5] After separating from the Hervormde Kerk in 1834, the churches of the Afscheiding had experienced steady growth: in 1849 they had about 40,000 souls, in 1874 they had 110,000 souls, and by 1889 they had 189,000 souls. Meanwhile, the Doleantie consisted of some who

---

5   For a complete treatment of this union, cf. Bouma, *Secession, Doleantie, and Union*, from which much of the following information is taken.

had remained in the mother church. Led by Abraham Kuyper, these "aggrieved ones" (*doleerende*) finally saw the apostasy in the Hervormde Kerk and left in 1886 with 200 congregations, 76 pastors, and 181,000 souls. They did not join with the Afscheiding churches but instead formed their own denomination. Nevertheless, both groups quickly came to realize that they had

Abraham Kuyper

much in common, and meetings were held to discuss unification.

In these initial discussions Van Velzen played an important role. The first meeting to be held between the two groups was on October 6, 1887, in the city of Utrecht. Representing the Doleantie group were F. L. Rutgers, W. van den Bergh, and Abraham Kuyper. Present for the Afscheiding churches were Helenius de Cock, D. K. Wielenga, and Simon van Velzen. Because he was the oldest man in attendance and

because of the tremendous respect that the other deputies had for him, Van Velzen was chosen to chair the meeting. The fruit of this first meeting was a set of twelve theses concerning the union that would serve as a springboard for future discussion.

The two parties met for a second time in Kampen on November 17, 1887, and again on February 17, 1888, in Amsterdam, with Van Velzen chairing both meetings. One issue that was raised at these meetings was the basis for union. Kuyper had proposed a set of thirty-one theses for union that was very speculative. In response, Van Velzen and Lucas Lindeboom proposed an alternative set of theses that "proceeded from the assumption that the discussions must take place only on the basis of the Reformed Confessional documents and by way of the clear statements within them." The two were convinced that "if there is to be any hope of blessing over the union, we must first return to Scripture and the Confession and from there seek the point and best manner for finding a true organic unity."[6] Van Velzen appealed to Kuyper and said, with tears in his eyes, "Beloved brother, we have our glorious, clear, tested Confession, and we must stick to it. Only on that basis may union be sought." Van Velzen's appeal was successful; Kuyper withdrew his proposed plan of union and agreed to seek union on the basis of the confessions.

After these initial meetings, Van Velzen did not participate directly in any further discussions. Due to his advanced age and increasing health problems, he was forced to watch from the sidelines.

The road to union was not without hurdles. In particular, one major hurdle was the titanic persona of Kuyper. A number of people in the Secession churches took issue with some of Kuyper's theological positions, and in their minds the reading of his works was anathema. The thought of uniting with him was difficult for them to envision.

Another obstacle was the differing views of the mother church. The Afscheiding churches claimed that the Hervormde Kerk was the false church, but the men of the Doleantie were not ready to say this even though they acknowledged her great weaknesses. Some questioned whether the two groups could truly be one if they maintained these opposing viewpoints.

A final major hangup was where to train men for the ministry. The Secession churches wanted their ministers trained at their seminary in Kampen, but the Doleantie wanted them trained at Kuyper's Free University in Amsterdam. Eventually,

---

6   Bouma, *Secession, Doleantie, and Union*, 55–56.

the two groups agreed to allow future ministers to be trained at either one.

After working through these differences, the official union between the two finally took effect on June 17, 1892, at a joint synodical meeting in Amsterdam. While the strong and capable churchmen from both sides were taking their seats, suddenly a hush fell over the large crowd. All eyes turned to see a rather unusual and unexpected sight: two strapping young men carrying in a chair on which was seated a very old man: Van Velzen. He had been insistent that he wanted to be present at such a momentous occasion.

So highly respected was he by those in attendance that he was known to all as "Father" van Velzen. The speakers that summer day all paid tribute to this beloved minister and professor. Willem H. Gispen, former catechumen of Van Velzen and president of the meeting for the Afscheiding churches, recognized the frailty of his former pastor and said, "I do not know what it is like in heaven, but if the saints talk with each other there and are interested in the struggle and joy of the church here on earth, then you must tell your former fellow battlers what you have seen here, and their joy will be great when you cry out to them: They are one!"[7]

Abraham Kuyper, presiding over the meeting for the Doleantie churches, added some touching words of his own: "In you, more than in any other, lies the seal of the historical unity and communion of our Churches."[8]

The delegates called for Van Velzen to speak, but he was too weak to stand and do so. However, his son Simon van Velzen III, a member of the Second Chamber of Parliament, spoke for him,

---

7   Quoted in Bouma, *Secession, Doleantie, and Union*, 210.
8   Quoted in Bouma, *Secession, Doleantie, and Union*, 210.

saying that his father considered this a "fulfilment of the great wish of his heart." So captivated was the audience by this man that a later news report recounted, "How simple and warm these proceedings were also became apparent when a voice was heard from the balcony asking that 'Father' van Velzen be placed in a different part of the church so that the people seated in the balcony would be able to get a look at him."[9]

The united group then sang "Father" van Velzen's favorite psalm, stanza two of Psalm 40:

A new and joyful song of praise
He taught my thankful heart to raise;
And many, seeing me restored,
Shall fear the Lord and trust;
And blest are they that trust the Lord,
The humble and the just.[10]

The new denomination took the name *Gereformeerde Kerken in Nederlands* (GKN—Reformed Churches in the Netherlands). The union brought together about 700 congregations, 425 pastors, and 370,000 members.

◆ ◆ ◆

As exciting as this union was for Van Velzen and those who were directly involved, not all were so thrilled. Three ministers (Frederik P. L. C. van Lingen, Philippus J. Wessels, and Johannes Wisse), three congregations, and about seven hundred members refused

9 Quoted in Bouma, *Secession, Doleantie, and Union*, 210–11.
10 No. 111:2, in *The Psalter with Doctrinal Standards, Liturgy, Church Order, and added Chorale Section*, reprinted and revised edition of the 1912 United Presbyterian *Psalter* (Grand Rapids, MI: William B. Eerdmans Publishing Co., 1927; rev. ed. 1995).

to join with the Doleantie and continued on separately as the CGK. Within a year, more members of the united denomination had left, and the CGK had grown to seventeen congregations. This denomination remains today and is a sister church of the Free Reformed Churches of North America.

Hindsight might lead the reader to question the wisdom of the union of Afscheiding and Doleantie—at least, the wisdom of uniting so quickly. Van Velzen's eagerness to unite on the sole basis of the Reformed confessions was an admirable beginning, but it did not take into account other major differences between the two groups.

The fact of the matter is that these were two very different groups of people. The Afscheiding churches were made up largely of poor, simple people. However, the Doleantie was made up largely of rich, well-educated people.

Major doctrinal differences also existed between the two groups, and in the haste to unite, these were not all worked through carefully and fully. The two sides failed to realize that they could both say they held to the Reformed confessions and yet interpret certain aspects of them differently.

There were especially four areas of doctrinal difference remaining between them. First, regarding justification, the Afscheiding generally maintained justification in time by faith while the Doleantie tended to emphasize eternal justification. Second, regarding regeneration, the Afscheiding taught mediate regeneration while the Doleantie argued for immediate regeneration. Third, regarding the ground of baptism, the Afscheiding said the ground for baptism is the promise of God while the Doleantie followed the thinking of Kuyper and said the ground for baptism is presupposed regeneration. Fourth, regarding the logical order of God's eternal decrees, the Afscheiding tended to be infralapsarian while the Doleantie were more supralapsarian.[11]

The result of this was a denomination that was united on paper but not in reality. Within the GKN were "A" churches (whose roots were in the Afscheiding) and "B" churches (whose roots were in the Doleantie). "A" churches maintained the distinctives of the Afscheiding and would never call a "B" minister. "B" churches maintained the distinctives of the Doleantie and would not think of calling an "A" minister.

The two sides in the denomination continued to debate these issues for years after the union was finalized. Eventually, they came together in an attempt to resolve some of these strong differences with the Conclusions of Utrecht in 1905.[12] However, that still did not bring about a settled peace in the GKN. Finally, the issues would come to a head in the 1940s with the deposition of Klaas Schilder and the formation of the GKN "Liberated." But that would be long after "Father" van Velzen passed to glory.

---

11 For more on these differences, cf. J. Mark Beach, "Abraham Kuyper, Herman Bavinck, and 'The Conclusions of Utrecht 1905,'" *Mid-America Journal of Theology*, 2008, no. 19:11–68.

12 For the text of the Conclusions of Utrecht, cf. J. L. Shaver, *The Polity of the Churches* (Chicago: Church Polity Press, 1947), 2:34–37.

Chapter 15

───◈───

THE SWORD
FOR THE SCEPTER

Throughout his long life, Van Velzen had seen many loved ones and colleagues brought to the grave. On June 2, 1888, he received one such piece of difficult news: Brummelkamp had died.

Van Velzen was asked to speak at the funeral of Brummelkamp on June 7, which was one of his last public speaking engagements. Deeply moved by the proceedings, he had to lean for support upon his son-in-law and a colleague.

From beginning to end, Van Velzen and Brummelkamp had an interesting relationship. They had fought together in the war with Belgium, they had grown up together as part of the Scholte Club, they had married into the same family, and together they had reformed the church. They did not always see eye-to-eye, and in fact were bitterly opposed to each other for years. Eventually, they made their peace, guided the churches as the two main leaders for many years, and lived out their last years as colleagues and brothers. Their lives were inextricably linked, as close as any two men who have ever lived. Now, Brummelkamp was gone. Van Velzen was alone, the last of the original reformers still living.

In certain respects, Van Velzen was a broken man after the death of Brummelkamp. He immediately went home and began destroying old letters and his personal papers. What was not destroyed by his own hand was destroyed after his death by his son-in-law on his orders. The specific reason is unknown, although generally he did so knowing that he also must soon die. Perhaps it was done out of humility, not wanting much ado made over him and his papers after his death.

After the funeral of his friend, Van Velzen spoke just a few times publicly. One of those times, he preached a sermon at the opening of the school year at Kampen in 1889 to his fellow professors and the ninety students enrolled that year. Appropriately, he preached from 2 Corinthians 4:7: "But we have this treasure in earthen vessels, that the excellency of the power may be of God, and not of us."[1] No one felt the truth of this passage more acutely than the aged speaker himself.

On December 18 of that year, just a few days after he turned eighty, he concluded his ninth term as rector of the school. Before handing over the rectorship to Helenius de Cock, he gave a speech, as was customary. Still the gifted speaker even in his twilight years, he addressed his beloved students from the heart without having any notes in front of him.

◆ ◆ ◆

By 1896, Van Velzen was clearly reaching the end of his earthly sojourn. When his children came to visit, Van Velzen expressed to them a desire only to be "with my books." He had an extensive library but still knew from long use where each book and paper was located. Just to be near them was a comfort to his soul.[2]

---

1 Van Gelderen, *Simon van Velzen*, 49.
2 Van Gelderen, *Simon van Velzen*, 55.

In his last days, he had occasion often to reflect upon the tumultuous years of his life and all that he had experienced. When asked how he was able to remain steadfast in the face of all the opposition and trouble, his answer was simple and beautiful: *"Wonderbare genade! Wonderbare genade!* (Wonderful grace! Wonderful grace!)"[3] He was a champion of God's sovereign grace to the end, knowing as he did from personal experience that sovereign grace of God working in him.

An older Simon van Velzen

On April 3, 1896, which was Good Friday, God finally called the old warrior to his eternal home at the age of eighty-six. How fitting that the man who spent his life preaching the gospel of the cross of Jesus Christ should be brought to be with his Savior on the day of the remembrance of his death on the cross. Van Velzen had left the church militant for the church triumphant, trading his sword for the scepter, as was his earnest longing. His body was laid to rest five days later, on April 8.[4]

◆ ◆ ◆

The significance of Simon van Velzen for the Reformed churches in the Netherlands was tremendous. He exerted as much influence

---

3 Quoted in Van Gelderen, *Simon van Velzen*, 55; Wormser, *Karakter en genade*, 173.

4 Van Gelderen, *Simon van Velzen*, 56. Wormser mistakenly gives the day of his death as April 8, but April 8 was a Wednesday, not a Friday, and was actually the day of his burial (cf. *Karakter en genade*, 174).

as (or very likely, *more than*) any of the other fathers of the Afscheiding. The influence of most of the others was limited. Hendrik de Cock was the unquestioned leader of the churches in the beginning, but he died at a young age in 1842, a mere eight years after the reformation began. George F. Gezelle Meerburg was a quiet man who did not exert much sway during the secession, and he too died relatively young in 1855. More influential was H. P. Scholte, but he fell out of favor with the reformers and their followers, grew more radical in his thinking, and finally left the Netherlands in 1847 to establish an independent church in Pella, Iowa. The influence of Albertus van Raalte was limited as well, because in 1846 he too immigrated to America to found the small colony of Holland, Michigan.

The only other father to have as significant of an impact on the churches as Van Velzen was Anthony Brummelkamp.[5] Like Van Velzen, Brummelkamp was involved in most of the major events in the history of the Afscheiding, although he did not live to see the union with the Doleantie. But the influence of Brummelkamp was not always positive. For one thing, he separated himself from the fellowship of the churches for a number of years, and when he finally returned, his influence was felt negatively on account of his promotion of the well-meant offer of the gospel.

The effect of Helenius de Cock on the churches was also immense, but he was not truly a father of the Afscheiding, not having entered the ministry until ten years after the secession.[6]

---

5   Melis te Velde argues in his biography of Brummelkamp that Brummelkamp was actually the most influential figure, more so even than Van Velzen. Cf. *Anthony Brummelkamp*, 17.

6   Herman Bavinck said of De Cock, "Without detracting at all from the merits of the other teachers with whom he joined the School in 1854, it may be freely stated that his influence on the formation of the students was the most powerful." Quoted in Veenhof, *Prediking en uitverkiezing*, 133.

Compared with all these men, Van Velzen had the most significant and positive influence on the churches of the Afscheiding. His life is essentially a history of this reformation—the beginning in 1834, the struggles in the early years, the joy of starting Kampen in 1854, and the union with the Doleantie in 1892. In all these events, Van Velzen played a significant role and left his mark on these churches. Although in the end the influence of Brummelkamp and Helenius de Cock won out, Van Velzen kept the denomination on the path of orthodoxy for many years.

An older Helenius de Cock

It seems strange, then, that Van Velzen remains largely unknown today. Most works on the Afscheiding mention him only briefly, and almost nothing has appeared in English on his life and work. Where he is mentioned, his influence is largely discredited on account of his forceful character. Dutch historian Harm Bouwman wrote, "Van Velzen was a man of great gifts and abilities, a man of broad classical education, of great learning, of knowledge and study." But he said also that just as Van Velzen's outward appearance was "long, thin, angular, and stiff, so too was he in his character. He had an inborn lust for polemics...furthermore he was unyielding, obstinate, and domineering."[7] P. Y. De Jong wrote similarly, "Simon Van Velzen was...a man of strong character and convictions whose zeal for the Reformed faith was not always exercised without blemish." Later, referring to a dispute in

---

7   Bouwman, *De crisis der jeugd*, 39.

which Van Velzen was involved, De Jong said, "Van Velzen was not above seeking for himself a powerful place" in the church.[8] Though he presented a more balanced view of Van Velzen, John Kromminga nevertheless concluded, "Van Velzen...had a tendency toward polemics that limited his influence."[9]

My hope is that the preceding pages have dispelled these negative evaluations of Van Velzen's life and influence. Despite his faults, Van Velzen was one of the most important fathers of the Afscheiding. He was more balanced than most assume, and when he did enter the polemical arena, he did so out of a conviction for the truth and a love for the churches he served. He was one of the most—if not *the* most—influential in this reformation movement. It is a mistake, therefore, to portray Van Velzen as a narrow-minded, obstinate, and domineering figure who had, as a result, very little impact.

The following analysis of W. De Graaf is more accurate than most:

> [Van Velzen] was a man who desired to maintain, defend, and develop the old Reformed theology. He held fast the line of the Reformation without deviating an inch. He succeeded after more than ten years of struggle [to start a seminary] to make this mark upon the churches of the Afscheiding...A man like Van Velzen was indispensable at that time...Thus he served as a rich blessing for the School and the Churches. Not incorrectly have some called him the Calvin-figure of the School.[10]

---

8 De Jong, "The Dawn of a New Day," 30, 34.
9 Kromminga, "'De Afscheiding'—Review and Evaluation," 48.
10 De Graaf, *Een monument der Afscheiding*, 57.

It is not too much to say then, as one source has, that "Van Velzen was the soundest, firmest, and most fiery of the ministers of the Secession. It is this kind of advocacy of the Reformed faith, particularly the sovereignty of grace, and this kind of Reformed minister that make the agony of a Secession or a *Doleantie* every 50 or 100 years unnecessary."[11] This is not to say that Van Velzen was blameless in his dealings with others or that he was always an easy person to get along with. It does affirm, however, the significant position he held in the Afscheiding churches.

In this light, we can better understand the character of the man. He was undoubtedly a very fiery personality and firm in his convictions. He often directed these qualities toward the reformation and preservation of the church, though there were certainly times as a young man, especially in the Amsterdam affair, where he exercised his zeal in a sinful way. However, despite his flaws, Van Velzen was driven by an earnest love for Christ's church and a desire for the glory of God.

This is also the judgment of one of his Dutch biographers. The biographer recognizes that many have hastily concluded that Van Velzen was "only a quarreler or schismatic." But he objects strongly: "On the contrary!" He argues that Van Velzen was "not reactionary." Rather, he says:

> A more complete biography [of Van Velzen] would, more than that of Brummelkamp, shed light on the main stream of the churches of the Afscheiding of 1834; if there has been anyone who—unyieldingly, stubbornly, obstinately—held fast to the historic line of the Reformed churches in the Netherlands, then it was he. By his leadership, his advice,

---

11 David J. Engelsma, review of *Secession, Doleantie, and Union: 1834–1892* by Hendrik Bouma, *Standard Bearer* 72, no. 9 (February 1, 1996): 214.

his driving sometimes, and also his publications, he held the course with a steady hand and ensured, humanly speaking, that after half a century a Christian Reformed Church had emerged.[12]

In the end, Van Velzen's greatest influence on the Dutch churches lay in the realm of preaching. He was a gifted preacher who devoted many decades of his life to preparing and delivering solid meat for the congregations he served. Then, when he was called from the active ministry to teach at the seminary, he devoted his time especially to molding his students into capable, faithful preachers. Van Gelderen agrees: "His chief work lay in the classroom where he endeavored to form good preachers."[13] From when he began teaching in 1854 until shortly after his death in 1896, there were 681 students in total enrolled at Kampen,[14] which means conservatively that Van Velzen had a hand in training more than 500 ministers in the Dutch Reformed churches. That kind of positive influence ought to be recognized.

Not only did Van Velzen have a great impact on the churches in the Netherlands, but he also had an impact overseas, particularly among the Dutch Reformed immigrants in Holland. When Van Raalte led his group of churches into the Reformed Church in America in 1850, not all were satisfied. A group finally split off in 1857 and formed what would later become the Christian Reformed Church. The leaders of this new denomination, particularly Rev. Koene Vanden Bosch and Elder Gysbert Haan, were influenced by Van Velzen prior to their coming to the United States. They were from Van Velzen's "conservative wing" and were

---

12 Van Gelderen, *Simon van Velzen*, 59–60.
13 Van Gelderen, *Simon van Velzen*, 61.
14 Van Gelderen, *Simon van Velzen*, 32.

some of the "sternest" Calvinists just as he was.[15] Van Velzen also garnered support for that fledgling group from the European side of the ocean. In time, many ministers trained by Van Velzen at Kampen crossed the ocean and became ministers in the CRC. This means that Reformed denominations in America, including the Christian Reformed Churches, the United Reformed Churches, and the Protestant Reformed Churches, can all trace their spiritual heritage to Van Velzen.

Gysbert Haan
(Image courtesy of Heritage Hall,
Calvin University, Grand Rapids, MI)

Simon van Velzen was a tireless and fearless defender of the faith, a true father of the Afscheiding. He was powerfully used by God to bring about reformation to the churches in the Netherlands, to preserve this reformation in the years that followed, and to pass on a rich doctrinal heritage to churches in his native land and in America.

---

15 Henry J. Beets, *The Christian Reformed Church in North America* (Grand Rapids, MI: Eastern Ave. Book Store, 1923), 46, 62. Pronk says that Haan "received elder training" from Van Velzen (cf. *A Goodly Heritage*, 332).

BIBLIOGRAPHY

Algra, H. *Het wonder van de 19e eeuw: Van vrije kerken en kleine luyden* [The miracle of the 19th century: of free churches and little people]. Franeker: T. Wever, 1976.

Baars, Arie. *The Secession of 1834*. Mitchell, Ontario: Free Reformed Publications, 2011.

Bangs, Carl. *Arminius: A Study in the Dutch Reformation*. Nashville, TN: Abingdon Press, 1971.

Beach, J. Mark. "Abraham Kuyper, Herman Bavinck, and 'The Conclusions of Utrecht 1905.'" *Mid-America Journal of Theology*, 2008, no. 19:11–68.

Beeke, Joel R. "The Dutch Second Reformation (*Nadere Reformatie*)." *Calvin Theological Journal* 28, no. 2 (November 1993): 298–327.

Beets, Henry. *The Christian Reformed Church in North America: Its History, Schools, Missions, Creed and Liturgy, Distinctive Principles and Practices and Its Church Government*. Grand Rapids, MI: Eastern Ave. Book Store, 1923.

Bos, F. L. "Velzen, Simon Van." *Biografisch lexicon voor de geschiedenis van het Nederlands protestantisme* [Biographical lexicon for the history of Dutch Protestantism], 2:431–33. Kampen: J. H. Kok, 1983.

Bouma, Hendrik. *Secession, Doleantie, and Union: 1834–1892*. Translated by Theodore Plantinga. Neerlandia, Alberta: Inheritance Publications, 1995.

Bouwman, Harm. *De crisis der jeugd: Eenige bladzijden uit de geschiedenis van de kerken der Afscheiding* [The crisis of youth: Some pages out of the history of the churches of the Secession]. Kampen: J. H. Kok, 1914.

Bratt, James D., *Abraham Kuyper: Modern Calvinist, Christian Democrat*. Grand Rapids, MI: William B. Eerdmans Publishing Co., 2013.

_____. *Dutch Calvinism in Modern America: A History of a Conservative Subculture*. Grand Rapids, MI: William B. Eerdmans Publishing Co., 1984.

Bruins, Elton J., Karen G. Schakel, Sara Fredrickson Simmons, and Marie N. Zingle. *Albertus and Christina: The Van Raalte Family, Home and Roots.* Holland, MI: A. C. Van Raalte Institute/Grand Rapids, MI: William B. Eerdmans Publishing Co., 2004.

Brummelkamp Jr., Anthony. *Levensbeschrijving van wijlen Prof. A. Brummelkamp* [Biography of the late Prof. A. Brummelkamp]. Kampen: J. H. Kok, 1910.

Dalhuysen, T. "De Afscheiding van S. van Velzen" [The secession of S. van Velzen]. *Troffel en Zwaard* [Trowel and sword], no. 5 (1902): 263–84. https://www.delpher.nl/nl/boeken/view?identifier=MMTUA01:000000 413:00003&query=dalhuysen+van+velzen+afscheiding&coll=boeken (accessed July 16, 2020).

De Graaf, W. *Een monument der Afscheiding: De Theologische Hogeschool van de Gereformeerde Kerken in Nederland 1854–1954* [A monument of the Secession: The Theological School of the Reformed Churches in the Netherlands, 1854–1954]. Kampen: J. H. Kok, 1955.

De Groot, Martijn. "Geruisloze verandering: Onderzoek naar de identiteit-sontwikkeling van de Gereformeerde Kerken in Nederland na de Vrijmaking (1944–1961)" ["Silent change: examination of the development of the identity of the Reformed Churches in the Netherlands after the Liberation (1944–1961)"]. Master's thesis, Theologische Universiteit Apeldoorn, 2010. https://hdc.vu.nl/nl/Images/groot.Masterscriptie_Geruisloze_verandering _tcm215-169525.pdf (accessed November 26, 2012).

De Jong, Peter Y. "The Rise of the Reformed Churches in the Netherlands." *Crisis in the Reformed Churches: Essays in Commemoration of the Great Synod of Dort, 1618–1619,* edited by Peter Y. De Jong, 17–37. Grandville, MI: Reformed Fellowship Inc., 2008.

De Jong, Peter Y. and Nelson D. Kloosterman, eds. *The Reformation of 1834: Essays in Commemoration of the Act of Secession and Return.* Orange City, IA: Pluim Publishing Inc., 1984.

Dosker, Henry E. *Levensschets van Rev. A. C. Van Raalte, D.D.* Nijkerk: C. C. Callenbach, 1893.

Eglinton, James. *Bavinck: A Critical Biography.* Grand Rapids, MI: Baker Academic, 2020.

Engelsma, David J., ed. *Always Reforming: Continuation of the Sixteenth-Century Reformation*. Jenison, MI: Reformed Free Publishing Association, 2009.

_____. *Covenant and Election in the Reformed Tradition*. Jenison, MI: Reformed Free Publishing Association, 2011.

_____. *Hyper-Calvinism and the Call of the Gospel: An Examination of the "Well-Meant Offer" of the Gospel*. 3rd ed. Jenison, MI: Reformed Free Publishing Association, 2014.

_____. "I Remember Herman Hoeksema: Personal Remembrances of a Great Man (10)." *Beacon Lights* 50, no. 7 (July 2009): 9–12.

_____. Review of *Secession, Doleantie, and Union: 1834–1892*, by Hendrik Bouma, *Standard Bearer* 72, no. 9 (February 1, 1996): 213–4.

_____. "The Courage of the Minister of the Word (concl.)." *Standard Bearer* 84, no. 21 (September 15, 2008): 490.

Engelsma, Joshua. "'Father' van Velzen: The Significance of Simon van Velzen for the Reformation of 1834," *Protestant Reformed Theological Journal* 46, no. 2 (April 2013): 3–47.

Faber, Jelle. *American Secession Theologians on Covenant and Baptism*. Neerlandia, Alberta/Pella, IA: Inheritance Publications, 1996.

Gleason, Ron. *Herman Bavinck: Pastor, Churchman, Statesman, and Theologian*. Phillipsburg, NJ: P & R Publishing, 2010.

Godfrey, W. Robert. "Calvin and Calvinism in the Netherlands." *John Calvin: His Influence in the Western World*, edited by W. Stanford Reid, 95–120. Grand Rapids, MI: Zondervan Publishing House, 1982.

Gritters, Barrett. "Who Will Train the Churches' Ministers?" *Standard Bearer* 91, no. 4 (November 15, 2014): 77–80.

Handelingen en verslagen van de Algemene Synoden van de Christelijk Afgescheidene Gereformeerde Kerk (1836–1869) met stukken betreffende de synode van 1843, bijlagen en registers [Acts and reports of the General Synods of the Christian Secession Reformed Church (1836–1869) with documents concerning the synod of 1843, appendices, and registers]. Houten/Utrecht: Den Hertog, 1984.

Hanko, Herman. *Portraits of Faithful Saints*. Grandville, MI: Reformed Free Publishing Association, 1999.

Harinck, George and Hans Krabbendam, eds. *Breaches and Bridges: Reformed Subcultures in the Netherlands, Germany, and the United States.* VU Studies on Protestant History 4, edited by J. de Bruijn and G. J. Schutte. Amsterdam: VU Uitgeverij, 2000.

Heideman, Eugene P. *Hendrik P. Scholte: His Legacy in the Netherlands and in America.* Grand Rapids, MI: William B. Eerdmans Publishing Co., 2015.

Hemkes, G. K. *Een man des volks: Het leven van Prof. Geert Egberts Boer naar aanteekeningen uit zijn dagboek* [A man of the people: the life of Prof. Geert Egberts Boer according to notes out of his diary]. Grand Rapids, MI: J. B. Hulst, 1904.

Hettema, Hette Piers. *Nagedachtenis en Levenservaringen, beschreven van H. P. Hettema, oud-ouderling te Beetgum* [Memory and life experiences, described by H. P. Hettema, former elder in Beetgum]. Leeuwarden, 1833.

Hulst, Lammert J. *Drie en zestig jaren prediker: Gedenkschriften van Ds. Lammert J. Hulst* [Sixty-three years a preacher: Memoirs of Rev. Lammert J. Hulst]. Grand Rapids: Eerdmans Sevensma, 1913.

Hyma, Albert. *Albertus C. Van Raalte and His Dutch Settlements in the United States.* Grand Rapids, MI: William B. Eerdmans Publishing Co., 1947.

Jacobson, Jeanne M., Elton J. Bruins, and Larry J. Wagenaar, *Albertus C. Van Raalte: Dutch Leader and American Patriot.* Holland, MI: Hope College, 1996

Kamps, Marvin. *1834: Hendrik de Cock's Return to the True Church.* Jenison, MI: Reformed Free Publishing Association, 2014.

Keizer, G. *De Afscheiding van 1834: Haar aanleiding, naar authentieke brieven en bescheiden beschreven* [The Secession of 1834: Her occasion, according to authentic letters and modest descriptions]. Kampen: J. H. Kok, 1934.

_____. "Een paar brieven van wijlen Prof. S. van Velzen" [A few letters of the late Prof. S. van Velzen]. *Gereformeerd Theologisch Tijdschrift* [Reformed Theological Journal] 20, no. 11 (March 1920): 397–414.

Kromminga, D. H. *The Christian Reformed Tradition: From the Reformation Till the Present.* Grand Rapids, MI: William Eerdmans Publishing Co., 1943.

Kromminga, John H. "'De Afscheiding' – Review and Evaluation." *Calvin Theological Journal* 20, no. 1 (April 1985): 43–57.

Lagerwey, Walter. "The History of Calvinism in the Netherlands." *The Rise and Development of Calvinism: A Concise History*, edited by John H. Bratt, 63–102. Grand Rapids, MI: William B. Eerdmans Publishing Co., 1959.

Marsden, George M. *Jonathan Edwards: A Life*. New Haven & London: Yale University Press, 2003.

Nyenhuis, Jacob E. and George Harinck, eds. *The Enduring Legacy of Albertus C. Van Raalte as Leader and Liaison*. The Historical Series of the Reformed Church in America 81. Holland, MI: A. C. Van Raalte Institute/Grand Rapids, MI: William B. Eerdmans Publishing Co., 2014.

Oostendorp, Lubbertus. *H. P. Scholte: Leader of the Secession of 1834 and Founder of Pella*. Franeker: T. Wever, 1964.

Pieters, Albertus. "Historical Introduction." *Classis Holland Minutes 1848–1858*. Grand Rapids, MI: Grand Rapids Printing Co., 1943.

Pieters, K. J. and J. R. Kreulen. *De kinderkoop volgens de beginselen der Gereformeerde Kerk in hare gronden, toedieningen en praktijk* [Infant baptism according to the principles of the Reformed Church in its grounds, administrations, and practice]. Franeker: T. Telenga, 1861.

Pronk, Cornelis. *A Goodly Heritage: The Secession of 1834 and Its Impact on Reformed Churches in the Netherlands and North America*. Grand Rapids, MI: Reformation Heritage Books, 2019.

Reenders, Hommo. "Albertus C. van Raalte: The *Homo Oecumenicus* among the Secession Leaders." *Calvin Theological Journal* 33, no. 2 (1998): 277–98.

Rullmann, J. C. *De Afscheiding in de Nederlandsch Hervormde Kerk der XIXe Eeuw* [The Secession in the Dutch Reformed Church of the 19th century]. 2nd ed. Amsterdam: W. Kirchner, 1916.

_____. "Velzen [Van]." In *Christelijke Encyclopaedie voor het Nederlandsche Volk* [Christian encyclopedia for the Dutch people]. Edited by F. W. Grosheide, J. H. Landwehr, C. Lindeboom, and J. C. Rullman, 5:544–45. Kampen: J. H. Kok.

Shaver, J. L. *The Polity of the Churches*. Vol. 2. Chicago: Church Polity Press, 1947.

Sheeres, Janet Sjaarda. *Son of Secession: Douwe J. Vander Werp*. The Historical Series of the Reformed Church in America 52. Grand Rapids, MI: William B. Eerdmans Publishing Co., 2006.

Sinnema, Donald. "The Origin of the Form of Subscription in the Dutch Reformed Tradition." *Calvin Theological Journal* 42, no. 2 (November 2007): 256–82.

Smilde, E. *Een eeuw van strijd over verbond en doop* [A century of conflict over covenant and baptism]. Kampen: J. H. Kok, 1946.

Smits, C. *De Afscheiding van 1834* [The Secession of 1834]. Vol. 3. Dordrecht: J. P. van den Tol, 1977.

_____. *De Afscheiding van 1834* [The Secession of 1834]. Vol. 5. Dordrecht: J. P. van den Tol, 1982.

Swierenga, Robert P. "1834 and 1857—Church Secessions and the Dutch Emigration." http://www.swierenga.com/Grafscap_pap.html (accessed September 11, 2013).

_____. "Van Raalte and Scholte: A Soured Relationship and Personal Rivalry." *Origins* 17, no. 1 (1999): 21–35.

Swierenga, Robert P. and Elton J. Bruins. *Family Quarrels in the Dutch Reformed Churches of the 19th Century.* The Historical Series of the Reformed Church in America 32. Grand Rapids, MI: William B. Eerdmans Publishing Co., 1999.

Te Velde, Melis, *Anthony Brummelkamp (1811–1888).* Barneveld: De Vuurbaak, 1988.

TenZythoff, Gerrit J. *Sources of Secession: The Netherlands Hervormde Kerk on the Eve of the Dutch Immigration to the Midwest.* The Historical Series of the Reformed Church in America 17. Grand Rapids, MI: William B. Eerdmans Publishing Co., 1987.

Tertullian, *Apology.* Vol. 3 of *The Ante-Nicene Fathers,* eds. Alexander Roberts and James Donaldson. Grand Rapids, MI: William B. Eerdmans Publishing Co., 1986.

Tjoelker, A. *Ds. S. van Velzen en zijn betekenis voor de Afscheiding in Friesland: Een kerk-hisorische bijdrage over de Jaren 1835–1840* [Rev. S. van Velzen and his significance for the Secession in Friesland: A church history contribution on the years 1835–1840]. Leeuwarden: A. Jongbloed, 1935.

Trimp, C. "S. van Velzen als prediker en homileet" ["S. van Velzen as preacher and homiletician"]. *Afscheiding-Wederkeer: Opstellen over de Afscheiding van 1834* [Secession-return: essays on the Secession of 1834], eds. D. Deddens and J. Kamphuis. Haarlem: Vijlbrief, 1984.

Vanden Berg, Frank. *Abraham Kuyper: A Biography.* St. Catherines, Ontario: Paideia Press, 1978.

Van der Zwaag, W. *Reveil en Afscheiding: Negentiende-eeuwse kerkhistorie met bijzondere actualiteit* [Reveil and Secession: Nineteenth century church history with a special theme]. Kampen: De Groot Goudriaan, 2006.

Van Gelderen, Jaap. *Simon van Velzen: Capita selecta* [Simon van Velzen: Select topics]. Kampen: Vereniging van Oud-Studenten van de Theologische Universiteit Kampen, 1999.

Van Oosterzee, J. J. *Practical Theology: A Manual for Theological Students,* trans. Maurice J. Evans. London: Hodder and Stoughton, 1878.

Van Raalte, Albertus C. *From Heart to Heart: Letters from the Rev. Albertus Christiaan Van Raalte to His Wife, Christina Johanna Van Raalte-De Moen, 1836–1847.* Edited by Leonard Sweetman. Translated by Egbert Ralph Post, Leonard Sweetman, and David Van Vliet. Grand Rapids, MI: Heritage Hall Publications, 1997.

Van Velzen, Simon. "The Apology of the Ecclesiastical Secession in the Netherlands, or A Letter to Mr. G. Groen Van Prinsterer regarding His Opinions Concerning the Secession and the Secessionists." Translated by Marvin Kamps. *Protestant Reformed Theological Journal* 45, no. 2 (April 2012): 30–67.

_____. *De zalige dooden, predicatie bij gelegenheid vna het afsterven van den weleerwaarden heer H. de Cock* [The blessedness of the dead, a sermon at the occasion of the decease of the highly esteemed pastor H. de Cock]. 's Gravenhage: J. van Golverdinge, 1842.

_____. Editorial comments on K. J. Pieters, "Eenige opmerkingen over de 69e vr. en antw. van den Katechismus ["Some remarks on the 69th question and answer of the Catechism"]. *De Bazuin* [The Trumpet] (May 19, 1865).

_____. "Episode uit den tijd der Kerkelijke Afscheiding in 1836" ["Episode out of the time of the ecclesiastical secession in 1836"]. *Avondstemmen van wijlen Prof. S. van Velzen* [Evening voices: essays of the late Prof. S. van Velzen]. Leiden: D. Donner, 1897. http://www.neocalvinisme.nl/dv/velzensv/svvavondstemmen.html#p12 (accessed July 16, 2020).

_____. *Gedenkschrift der Christelijke Gereformeerde Kerk, bij Vijftig-jarig Jubilé, 14 October 1884* [Memorial of the Christian Reformed Church, at the fifty-year anniversay, 14 October 1884]. Kampen: G.Ph. Zalsman, 1884. http://www.neocalvinisme.nl/tekstframes.html (accessed July 16, 2020).

_____. "Het verbond der verlossing" ["The covenant of redemption"]. *De Bazuin* [The Trumpet] (January 20, 1865).

_____. *Stem eens wachters op Zions muren* [Voice of a watchman on Zion's walls]. *Kompleete uitgave van de officiëele stukken betreffende den uitgang uit het Nederl. Herv. Kerkgenootschap* [Complete edition of the official documents concerning the exit from the Dutch Reformed Denomination]. Vol. 2. 2nd ed. Kampen: S. van Velzen Jr., 1863. https://babel.hathitrust. org/cgi/pt?id=hvd.ah5w4j&view=1up&seq=9 (accessed July 16, 2020).

Veenhof, C. *Prediking en uitverkiezing: Kort overzicht van de strijd, gevoerd in de Christelijk Afgescheidene Gereformeerde Kerk tusschen 1850 en 1870, over de plaats van de leer der uitverkiezing in de prediking* [Preaching and election: Brief overview of the struggle fought in the Christian Secession Reformed Church between 1850 and 1870 over the place of the doctrine of election in preaching]. Kampen: J. H. Kok, 1959.

Veldman, Harm. *Hendrik de Cock (1801–1842): Op de breuklijnen in theologie en kerk in Nederland* [Hendrik de Cock (1801–1842): on the fault lines in theology and church in the Netherlands]. Kampen: J. H. Kok, 2009.

Wagenaar, Lutzen H. *Het "Reveil" en de "Afscheiding": Bijdrage tot de Nederlandsche kerkgeschiedenis van de eerste helft der XIX eeuw* [The "Reveil" and the "Secession": A contribution to Dutch church history of the first half of the nineteenth century]. Heerenveen: J. Hepkema, 1880.

Wesseling, Jan. *De Afscheiding van 1834 in Friesland* [The Secession of 1834 in Friesland]. 3 vols. Groningen: De Vuurbaak, 1981.

Wormser, J. A. *In twee werelddeelen: Het leven van Albertus Christiaan Van Raalte* [On two continents: The life of Albertus Christiaan Van Raalte]. Vol. 1 of *Een schat in aarden vaten* [A treasure in earthen vessels]. Nijverdal: E. J. Bosch, 1915.

_____. *Karakter en Genade: Het Leven van Simon van Velzen* [Character and grace: the life of Simon van Velzen]. Vol. 4 of *Een schat in aarden vaten* [A treasure in earthen vessels]. Nijverdal: E. J. Bosch, 1916.

Wormser, J. A., and J. C. Rullmann. *Ernst en vrede: Het leven van George Frans Gezelle Meerburg* [Serious and peaceful: The life of George Frans Gezelle Meerburg]. Vol. 5 of *Een schat in aarden vaten* [A treasure in earthen vessels]. Baarn: E. J. Bosch, 1919.

INDEX

Riedel, F. Bekius, 67

"Robbers Synod," 141

Roman Catholic Church, 16, 25

Roorda, T., 21

Rotterdam (Belgium), 29, 101

Rottum (Groningen), 98

Rouveen (Netherlands), 116

Rutgers, F. L., 196

S

Sacramentarian phase, 16

Schilder, Klaas, 185, 201

Schivink, S. D., 81

Scholte, Hendrik Pieter, 21–22, 26–
27, 31, 34, 38, 40, 51, 55, 61,
62, 83, 90, 91, 100, 106, 107,
108, 109–110, 111, 112, 113,
119, 120–123, 127, 128–129,
130–133, 140, 141, 146, 147,
148, 158, 191, 206

Scholte Club, 31, 38–39, 40, 42,
53, 203

Schotsman, Nicholas, 18

Schouwenberg, A., 117

Scotland, 189

Secession (1848), 83, 85, 89, 93,
99, 103, 105, 124, 153, 165

Secession churches, 147, 177, 185,
186–187, 188, 189–190, 197

Secession Synod of 1849, 187

second Amsterdam dispute, 128

Second Chamber of Parliament, 198

Sexbierum/Harlingen (Friesland), 78

's-Hertogenbosch (Netherlands), 194

Sletskemoei, 57

Silesia, 52

Sinnema, Donald, 65

Sjoukjemoei, 57

Smilde, E., 182–183

Smitt, Wolter Wagter, 117, 193

Sneek (Friesland), 78, 80, 92, 98

South Holland, 23, 91, 110, 141

Spain, 13, 17, 33

Spoelstra, Sietske Geerts, 79

Stadtholder, 13

States General, 13

Storm, Sjouke, 79

St. Pterskerk, 29, 42

Stratingh, Zwaantje, 135, 193

Suringar, Lucas, 34, 35

Swierenga, Robert, 63–64, 142–143

Switzerland, 39

Synodical Board of the Hervormde
Kerk, 70–71

Synod of 1836, 95, 97, 109, 112

Synod of 1837, 115, 122

Synod of 1840, 139, 140, 144

Synod of 1843, 141

Synod of 1846, 160

Synod of 1851, 187

Synod of 1854, 155, 160–161, 172

Synod of 1857, 173

Synod of 1860, 174

Synod of 1869, 188

Synod of 1875, 163

Synod of 1882, 194

Synod of Dordt, 13, 17, 18, 37, 65

Synod of Franeker, 182

Synod of Groningen (1846), 144